VISUAL QUICKSTART GUIDE

PAGEMAKER 6.5

FOR WINDOWS

TED ALSPACH

 Peachpit Press

Visual QuickStart Guide
PageMaker 6.5
for Windows
Ted Alspach

Peachpit Press
2414 Sixth Street
Berkeley, CA 94710
(510) 548-4393
(510) 548-5991 (fax)
(800) 283-9444
Find us on the World Wide Web at:
http://www.peachpit.com
Peachpit Press is a division of Addison Wesley Longman

ISBN: 0-201-69650-9

0 9 8 7 6 5 4 3 2 1

Printed and bound in the United States of America

About the Author

Ted Alspach is the author of more than a dozen books on desktop publishing and graphics, as well as hundreds of articles on related topics.

Ted is the owner of Bezier Inc., located in the untamed desert somewhere in the middle of Arizona.

Please send any comments regarding this book to Ted at:

PageMakerVQS@bezier.com

and please visit VectorVille, a site dedicated to vector graphics, at:

http://www.bezier.com/vectorville

Other books by Ted Alspach

PageMaker 6.5 for Macintosh: Visual QuickStart Guide

Illustrator Effects Magic

Illustrator 7 Studio Secrets

Illustrator 7 Bible

Acrobat 3 for Macintosh and Windows: Visual QuickStart Guide

*Photoshop Complete**

KPT Studio Secrets[††]

Macworld Illustrator 6 Bible

Illustrator Filter Finesse[†]

*The Mac Internet Tour Guide, 2nd Ed.**

Microsoft Bob[†] *(I know, I know)*

Internet E-mail Quick Tour

The Complete Idiot's Guide to Photoshop

The Complete Idiot's Guide to QuarkXPress

Macworld Illustrator 5.0/5.5 Bible

*With other contributors   †with Jennifer Alspach   ††with Steven Frank

Acknowledgements

Many individuals contributed to this book in some way or another:

Nancy Davis, my wonderful editor at Peachpit.

Scott Calamar at LightSpeed Publishing.

Jennifer Alspach, my favorite up-and-coming author.

Rob Teeple, who made sure everything in this book works perfectly.

Sandee Cohen, who has some of the best VQS's out there (FreeHand and KPT).

And finally, everyone at Peachpit Press who helped move this book along until it hit paper.

Colophon

This book was created using:

Adobe PageMaker 6.5

Adobe Photoshop 4.0

Extensis PageTools 2.0.1

Flash-It! 3.0.2

Adobe Illustrator 7.0

Extensis VectorTools 2.0

UMAX S900L/200

Pentium 200mhz MMX with Win95

Adobe Garamond was used for the body copy, and Futura Extra Black Condensed was used to create the headings.

Book Design: Ted Alspach
Editor: Nancy Davis
Copy Editor: Scott Calamar, LightSpeed Publishing
Technical Editor: Robert Teeple
Index: Rebecca Plunkett

TABLE OF CONTENTS

PREFERENCES

5

PART II: TYPE

TYPE OBJECTS

6

CHARACTERS

7

PARAGRAPHS AND TABS

8

STYLES

9

PART III: GRAPHICS

DRAWING

10

PLACING IMAGES

11

WORKING WITH PHOTOSHOP AND ILLUSTRATOR

12

PHOTOSHOP FILTERS

13

COLORING

14

PART IV: LAYOUT

TEXT FLOW & THE STORY EDITOR

15

OBJECT MANAGEMENT

16

LAYERS

17

PART V: FINISHING

PRINTING

PART VI: APPENDIXES

GLOSSARY

WHAT'S NEW IN PAGEMAKER 6.5

EXTENSIS PAGETOOLS 2.0

INDEX

INTRODUCTION

It's easy to be intimidated by PageMaker's vast array of palettes, menus, and dialog boxes. Even if you have some idea of what you're supposed to be doing, just *finding* the correct command or dialog box can be an exercise in futility.

That's where this book comes in handy. It covers each of the most common tasks that you'll want to take on in PageMaker, along with some useful techniques that you might not even have imagined. Each task is presented in the most basic format possible, so newbies to PageMaker can read each step and refer to the accompanying figure, while experts can skim the text looking for just the information they need. Teachers can use this book as their students follow along, step by step, with each technique.

How to use this book

If you've never used a Visual QuickStart Guide from Peachpit Press (of which there are dozens, covering every major software package), then you'll be pleasantly surprised. This book takes you on a whirlwind tour of PageMaker 6.5, in a format that is both easy to understand, and fun to read. Examples are presented so you can follow along on your computer, comparing what you see on screen to the pictures on each page. All of the typical tasks for which you would use PageMaker are included, as well as other, not-so-common ones that you'll find useful when you move beyond the basics.

The book is designed so that if you were to read it from front to back, you could do so without having to do any flipping or cross referencing.

Most of the examples are presented in the following fashion:

To work through an example:

1. **Find the appropriate topic in the table of contents, the index, or by flipping through the pages looking at the thumb tabs.**

   The bold text (above) tells you what to do. The regular text below it (what you're reading right now) tells you what happens when you do it, or supplementary information you may find useful.

2. **Go to the page where the example appears.**

   I've kept the page numbers nice and big in the lower outside corner of each page to make finding topics easier.

3. **Read that example's steps.**

4. **At your computer, go through the steps one by one, following the directions on each page.**

   Most of the pages contain just one task with several illustrations and screenshots. The pages before and after each example contain related topics that you might find helpful.

PageMaker is fun

One of the real treats about writing this book was that I was able do almost all the work right in PageMaker. In fact, this entire book was designed, created, and laid out in PageMaker, allowing me to use real-world examples for each of the techniques you'll see presented.

While PageMaker is a huge program with a multitude of options, digging in and actually creating a page or two can be quite enjoyable. You'll find that the hours just slip by as you play around with layout, kerning your headlines just right, and giving your documents the little extra pizazz that makes them stand out from the norm.

Enjoy yourself!

PART I

BASICS

PageMaker. Makin' pages. The assembly of text and graphics into some semblance of order is what PageMaker is all about. PageMaker provides tools intended for this purpose, making the world of page layout easier and more enjoyable than ever before.

If you've never used page layout software before, if you're finally venturing into the medium of electronic publishing from a long history of traditional layout and typesetting, or if you just want to produce some really cool-looking pages, this is the chapter you should read before any other.

Even if you are familiar with other software, like QuarkXPress, you'll find the answers to many questions in the following pages.

Introduction to PageMaker

Page layout theory

PageMaker is a *page layout* program. The idea behind page layout is that either you or one of your minions has already done the tedious work of research, gathering graphics, writing text, and now you want to put all this stuff together on a page. Or several pages. Or a book. Or a magazine. Or a print ad. Or a web page.

PageMaker is the final stop on your journey for print publications, and your second-to-last stop for online documents. Here is where you place text and graphics side by side, a page at a time, until your publication is complete (**Figure 1**).

To save a PageMaker document for the first time:

1. Choose File->Save (Figure 11).

Or press Ctrl+S.

The Save Publication dialog box will appear (**Figure 12**).

(If you've previously saved the document, the Save command will overwrite your existing saved file, updating any changes you have made since the last time you saved.)

2. In the Save Publication dialog box, type the name of the document you're saving.

Be as descriptive as possible using the standard 8.3 naming conventions. If the document will only be used on WIN95 systems, use as many characters as needed.

3. In the Save Publication dialog box, set the location where the file should be saved.

By default, PageMaker will attempt to save your file in the PageMaker application directory. Don't let it do this. Instead, pick a directory (or create one) that contains other documents or nothing else.

4. Click the Save button.

The document will be saved.

Figure 1. Text and graphics are combined to form a PageMaker page.

Figure 2. The text that appears to the right, as shown in Microsoft Word.

Word processing prior to PageMaker

Text in PageMaker documents can be created directly within PageMaker, or it can be imported from a word processor. Word processors such as Microsoft Word and WordPerfect have additional word processing features that aren't found in PageMaker. When you create your text in a word processor, it must be saved in a format for importing into PageMaker, or copied from the word processor and pasted into a PageMaker document. **Figure** 2 shows this text (prior to editing) as it appears in a Microsoft Word document.

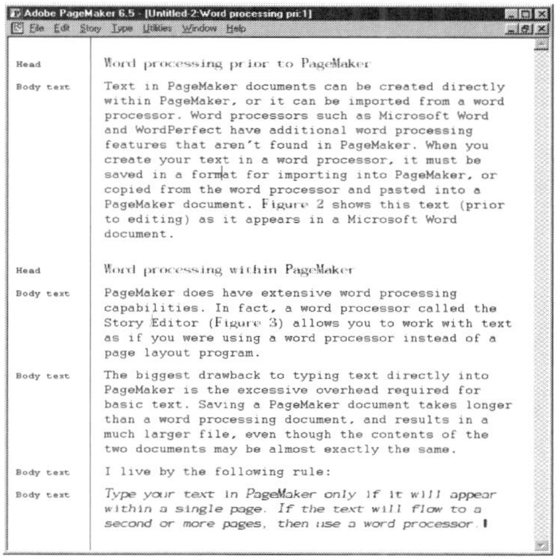

Word processing within PageMaker

PageMaker does have extensive word processing capabilities. In fact, a word processor called the Story Editor (**Figure 3**) allows you to work with text as if you were using a word processor instead of a page layout program.

The biggest drawback to typing text directly into PageMaker is the excessive overhead required for basic text. Saving a PageMaker document takes longer than a word processing document, and results in a much larger file, even though the contents of the two documents may be almost exactly the same.

I live by the following rule:

Type your text in PageMaker only if it will appear within a single page. If the text will flow to a second or more pages, then use a word processor.

Figure 3. The text that appears to the right, in PageMaker's Story Editor.

Importing graphics into PageMaker

You can place graphics saved in a variety of file formats into your PageMaker document. All the popular formats are supported, including EPS, TIF, BMP, WMF, JPEG, and GIF. You can create these graphics in other programs such as Adobe Photoshop or Adobe Illustrator. PageMaker even imports native Adobe Illustrator files.

Most of the images you see in this book, from screen shots to artwork, were edited in Adobe Photoshop before they were placed on each page. PageMaker can make limited modifications to placed images, such as cropping, scaling, rotating, and other effects. **Figure 4** shows what happens when an image is inverted within PageMaker. Image Control is discussed in Chapter 11.

Creating graphics within PageMaker

PageMaker allows you to create a limited variety of graphics, by drawing basic shapes and lines and filling and stroking them with different colors. **Figure 5** shows several images created solely with PageMaker's drawing tools.

Figure 4. This photograph was placed in PageMaker looking quite normal, and then PageMaker's Image Control dialog box was used to invert it.

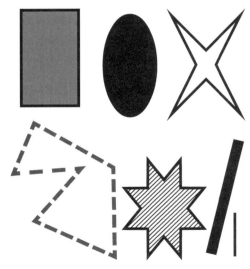

Figure 5. These images were created entirely within PageMaker using the built-in drawing tools.

Figure 6. The chapter opening page style for this book, created in PageMaker.

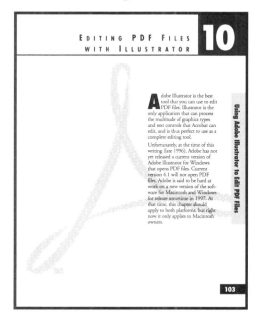

Figure 7. The chapter opening page for my Acrobat 3 Visual QuickStart Guide, *created in QuarkXPress.*

Designing with PageMaker

PageMaker is an extremely powerful design tool. So powerful, in fact, that it lets would-be designers actually design. And designers who have spent years perfecting their sense of design can take matters into their own hands, instead of leaving the actual execution up to layout artists, typesetters, and prepress operators.

However, PageMaker does not a good designer make, as Yoda would say. This book is peppered with design tips and ideas, but it certainly can't take the place of good old-fashioned design sense. I'm no artist, but I did study art (I would have had a minor if it wasn't for my stubborn refusal to take two additional art history classes). I've found that many basic design concepts and theories have been extremely useful as I've used PageMaker during the last 10 years.

Fortunately, design is largely subjective, so you can feel free to like my design while someone else may think it's as lame as a five-legged spider.

Figures 6 and 7 show my design of the chapter opening pages of this book (**Figure 6**) and another Visual QuickStart Guide I've done for Peachpit Press, on Adobe Acrobat (**Figure 7**). The Adobe Acrobat chapter opener was done in QuarkXPress, while the PageMaker chapter was done in, heh, well, I'll let you figure that out.

Design and Designers

Installing PageMaker

2

PageMaker's installation process is enough to scare most people away from ever actually using the program. While the Aldus installer has been finally removed from PageMaker, ugly remnants of it have been left behind, making the installation process more overwhelming than it needs to be.

Even the most basic installation can confuse seasoned computer-using veterans. This chapter will lead you through the installation process step by step, with emphasis on those areas that might be a little "much."

In addition, this chapter will take you through the installation of Acrobat Reader, so you can create and view PDF files with PageMaker.

Introduction to Installing

To install PageMaker:

1. Insert the PageMaker CD-ROM into your CD-ROM drive.

   The PM6.5 Autoplay window will appear on your screen (**Figure 1**).

   If you don't have a CD-ROM drive, Adobe has a floppy disk version of PageMaker available. Be aware, however, that it takes the better part of an hour to install PageMaker via floppy disks.

2. Click on "Install PageMaker 6.5."

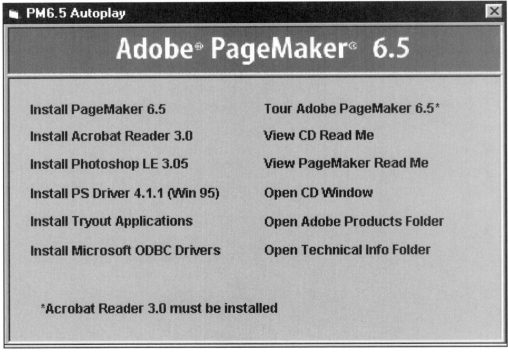

Figure 1. The PM6.5 Autoplay window.

Figure 2. The Installation title screen.

The installation title screen (**Figure 2**) will appear.

3. **Click the Title screen once.**

   The Welcome screen will appear (**Figure 3**).

4. **Click the Next button.**

   The Language Selection screen will appear.

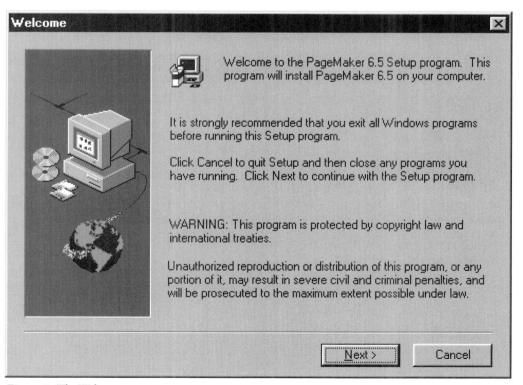

Figure 3. The Welcome screen.

5. **Click on your language in the Language Selection screen and click the Next button.**

   The Setup Type screen will appear (**Figure 4**).

6. **Choose the type of setup you would like.**

   I'd recommend that you install the Typical setup the first time you install PageMaker.

7. **Click the Next button.**

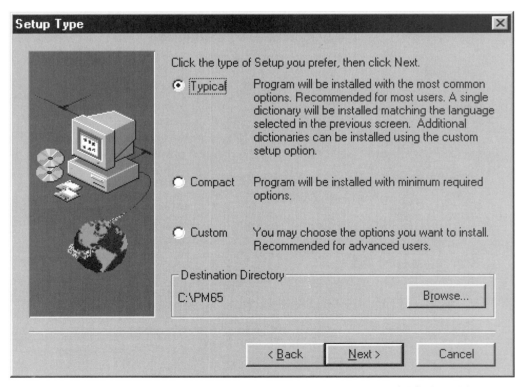

Figure 4. The Setup Type screen.

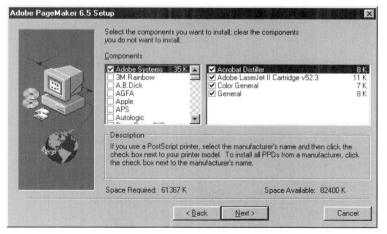

Figure 5. Choose the Printer manufacturer on the left, and the printer model on the right.

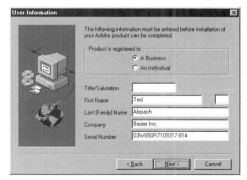

Figure 6. The User Information screen.

After a few seconds, a window listing components will appear. From the left list, choose the printer manufacturer of your printer. From the right list, choose the specific printer you want to use (**Figure 5**).

8. **Click the Next button**

   The User Information screen will appear (**Figure 6**).

9. **Enter your name, company, and serial number in the spaces provided.**

   If you aren't registering PageMaker as a business, choose the individual option (which grays out the Company name).

   Your serial number can be found on the CD-ROM sleeve (the cardboard envelope it came in) and on your registration card. Don't enter the one shown in Figure 6; the number shown is not a valid serial number and will not allow you to install PageMaker.

   (continued on the next page)

Installing PageMaker

10. **Click the Next button.**

    The registration confirmation screen appears.

11. **Verify that the information you entered is correct, then click the Yes button.**

    The installation will finally begin to take place, with a variety of screens appearing (like the one in **Figure** 7), extolling the virtues of PageMaker 6.5.

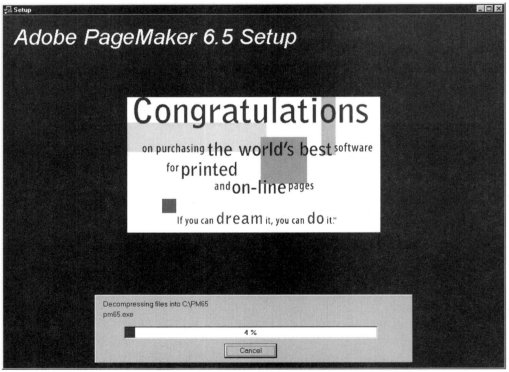

Figure 7. One of the promotional screens that appears during the installation process. If you had second thoughts about buying PageMaker, this dialog box should dispel them for good.

Figure 8. This box tells you that QuickTime 2.1 for Windows will be installed next.

Figure 9. Click the Finish button to end the installation process.

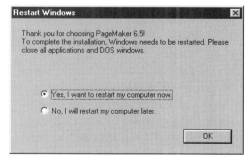

Figure 10. Click the OK button to restart your system.

Once the installation is complete (it takes roughly two to five minutes for installation, depending on your computer and CD-ROM drive), you'll be presented with a dialog box (**Figure 8**) that tells you the installer will be installing Apple QuickTime 2.1 for Windows.

12. **Click the OK button.**

    The ATM Installer window will appear.

13. **Click the Install button.**

    The Setup window will return, asking you if you want to register PageMaker at this time (**Figure 9**).

    The questionnaire is lengthy, so if you want to dig in and start using PageMaker right away, uncheck the PageMaker 6.5 online registration box.

14. **Click the Finish button.**

    The Restart Windows screen will appear (**Figure 10**). You should always restart windows after installing PageMaker.

15. **Click the OK button.**

    Windows will restart automatically.

Installing PageMaker

Color Management Device Profiles

One of the biggest problems with desktop publishing and graphics systems and software is the variation in color that can occur between original artwork (photos), the way it appears after being scanned in and placed in PageMaker, and how it appears when printed. There are other related issues as well, such as how colors you've selected from the Colors palette will match the final output.

The concept behind color device management is that each device displays color differently, but in a way that can be predicted. PageMaker's profiles can be used to help reduce the difference between original art, what appears on screen, and the final printed image. By installing profiles for each device you'll be using, you are in effect adjusting the way images are displayed and printed based on the way a particular brand and model of device displays or prints an object.

The Color Management Device Profiles installation window provides a few customizable options. If you aren't sure which brand or model you'll be using, you can check the main checkbox for each type of device. If you know what monitor you have, however, you can select only that monitor by clicking on the triangle to the left of the Monitor Profiles checkbox and choosing your monitor from the list.

TIPS AND TRICKS

If you aren't sure if Color Management Device Profiles are necessary or not, go ahead and install them. You can always dump the files if you decide not to use them, and they don't take up that much space on your hard drive.

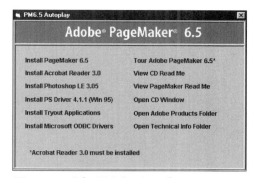

Figure 11. *The PM 6.5 Autoplay screen.*

Other Installation Options

When you insert the CD-ROM, the Autoplay screen (**Figure 11**) appears, providing many more options than just installing PageMaker. You can also install Acrobat Reader 3.0 (instructions for doing this are on the following pages), Photoshop LE 3.05 (a stripped-down version of Adobe Photoshop 3.0; the current version is 4.0), PS Driver (for printing to PostScript devices from Windows), Tryout Applications (crippled versions of Adobe software), and Microsoft ODBC Drivers.

You can also choose to Tour PageMaker 6.5 (you'll need Acrobat installed prior to doing this), which is a PDF document that shows you some of the basics of using PageMaker. From the Autoplay screen you can also view the Read Me files.

Other Installation Options

Acrobat Reader 3.0 is software that allows you to read PDF files, a universal cross-platform file type that PageMaker in particular excels at creating.

To install Acrobat Reader:

1. **Insert the PageMaker CD-ROM in your CD-ROM drive.**

   The PM 6.5 Autoplay window will appear (**Figure 12**).

2. **Click once on "Install Acrobat Reader 3.0."**

   This will launch the installation software.

2. **Click the Next button when the Welcome screen appears.**

3. **Click the Yes button on the Software License Agreement screen.**

   The installer will select a location on your hard drive automatically, and display the directory path in the Destination Directory section of the Choose Destination dialog box (**Figure 13**).

4. **To change the directory, click the Browse button. If the directory is correct, click the Next button.**

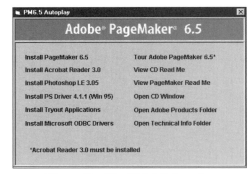

Figure 12. *The PM 6.5 Autoplay screen.*

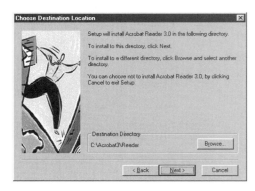

Figure 13. *Choose the destination directory of the Acrobat Reader software here.*

 **TIPS AND TRICKS**

You can learn more about Acrobat Reader (as well as the other components of Acrobat—Distiller and Exchange) by picking up a copy of *Acrobat 3 Visual QuickStart Guide* by Ted Alspach.

As Acrobat Reader installs itself, a progress bar fills in from left to right. You can stop the installation at any time by clicking the Cancel button.

5. **After installation, click the Finish button.**

6. **Click OK in the dialog box that follows.**

   The Installer will then quit.

7. **Verify Acrobat Reader has been installed properly by opening the directory where it was installed.**

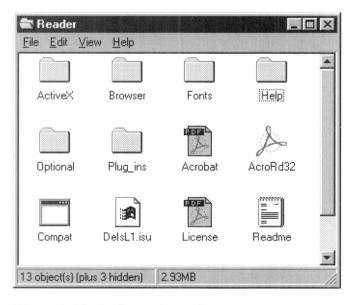

Figure 14. The Acrobat Reader window.

3

WORKING WITH PAGEMAKER FILES

There's no better way to get started using PageMaker than by looking at how to create new documents, how to save them, how to close them, and finally, how to open those documents that have been created, saved, and closed.

The contents of this chapter are critical because you'll be doing these things *every single time* you use PageMaker. Take the time to absorb this chapter fully; everything from this point on requires you to be very familiar with how to use PageMaker files.

In addition to the basics, I've included boatloads of tips on how to be as productive as possible while you're creating, saving, closing, and opening your documents.

To launch PageMaker:

Choose Adobe PageMaker 6.5 from the Start menu (Figure 1).

By default, Adobe stores it in the PageMaker 6.5 directory.

When PageMaker is launched in this way, no documents are opened, and no new document is created. Instead, you're given an empty application window. **Figure 2** shows what my screen looks like when I launch PageMaker.

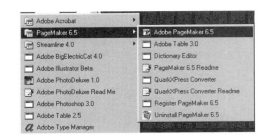

Figure 1. Choose Adobe PageMaker 6.5 from the Start menu.

Figure 2. My screen when I first launch PageMaker.

Launching PageMaker

Figure 3. Select New from the File menu.

Figure 4. The Document Setup dialog box.

To create a new document:

1. **Choose File⇨New (Figure 3).**

   Or press Ctrl+N.

   This will display the Document Setup dialog box (**Figure 4**).

2. **Enter any changes in the Document Setup dialog box and press the OK button.**

   A new document called Untitled 1 will appear on your screen with the entire first page of the document displayed in the document window (**Figure 5**).

   Document Setup options can be found on the following pages.

Figure 5. A new document as it first appears in PageMaker.

TIPS AND TRICKS

You don't ever need to actually "see" the Document Setup dialog box if you know the current settings will work with the new document you're creating. Just press Ctrl+N and then press the Enter key. The new document appears instantly.

Creating a New Document

The Document Setup dialog box

This dialog box (**Figure 6**) is probably the most crucial one in all of PageMaker, as it determines the way your document appears. Following are descriptions of each of the sections within the Document Setup dialog box. Step-by-step instructions on setting the values and choosing the options can be found on the next several pages.

Page size

The Page size pop-up menu lets you select from several different pre-defined page sizes. Changing this pop-up menu automatically changes the values in the Dimensions text fields, below the Page size menu.

Dimensions

If you want a page size that isn't listed in the Page size pop-up menu, you can enter the size of the page in these two text fields. Changing the values to something other than one of the preset values automatically changes the Page size pop-up menu to read "Custom." This helps prevent potential confusion after you've entered 18 inches by 4 inches (bumper sticker size), so that the Page size pop-up doesn't read "Letter."

Orientation

Tall makes the longer edge the vertical dimension, while Wide makes it the horizontal dimension.

Options

The following four options determine characteristics of multiple page documents. If your document consists of just a single page, ignore these settings.

Double-sided creates left and right pages, each of which appears separately when viewed in PageMaker.

Facing pages shows left and right pages together in PageMaker. This option is only available when Double-sided is checked.

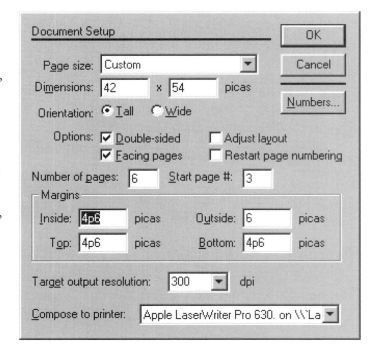

Figure 6. The invaluable Document Setup dialog box.

Adjust layout is only available once the document has been created. This option will actually reflow the text boxes and graphics to fit a new page size.

Restart page numbering only affects PageMaker documents used within book publications, and resets the page number to the Start page # value, regardless of its position within a book.

Number of pages

This function lets you specify the number of pages within your document. If you'll be using the Autoflow capabilities of PageMaker to add additional pages, keep the value at 1.

Start page

This option provides a new page number for the first page of the document. For instance, this chapter started on page 21, so I entered 21 in the Start page # text field.

Margins

The margin values set here are really margin *guides,* which can help you when you're designing your pages. The Inside and Outside text fields change to "Left" and "Right" when the Double-sided option is not checked.

Target output resolution

This is the setting that determines the resolution of the final printout of your document.

Compose to Printer

Choose the printer you plan on printing to here.

OK button

Clicking this button (or pressing Enter or Return) puts these document settings into effect.

Cancel button

Clicking this button (or pressing ESC) exits the dialog box without creating a new document or making changes to an existing one.

Numbers

This button brings up the Numbers dialog box, where you can set the style of page numbers.

TIPS AND TRICKS

Press Tab to go to the next text field (in dialog boxes), and Shift-Tab to go to the previous one.

Using the Document Setup Dialog Box

25

To set the size of your document:

1. **Choose File⇨New (Figure 7).**

   The Document Setup dialog box (**Figure 8**) will appear.

   If the document has already been created, choose File⇨Document Setup (Ctrl+Shift+P).

2. **Change the Page size pop-up menu to reflect the desired page size.**

   If the page size you want to use isn't listed, or if you want to create a page with dimensions that are different from the pop-up choices, enter the dimensions of the page into the Dimensions text fields.

3. **Click the OK button.**

   The document will be created (or changed) to reflect the size you have chosen.

To set the orientation to Tall:

In the Document Setup dialog box, select the Tall radio button and click OK.

The longer of the two dimensions will be vertical.

To set the orientation to Wide:

In the Document Setup dialog box, select the Wide radio button and click OK.

The longer of the two dimensions will be horizontal.

Figure 7. Select New from the File menu.

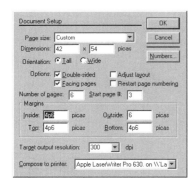

Figure 8. The Document Setup dialog box.

TIPS AND TRICKS

Changing the orientation will actually "swap" the two values in the Dimensions text fields. Most people tend to refer to area measurements as "such and such by such and such," with the first such and such meaning the width (horizontal measurement), and the second such and such referring to the height (vertical measurement).

Figure 9. Select Document Setup from the File menu.

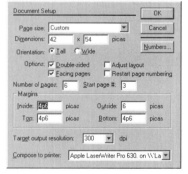

Figure 10. The Document Setup dialog box.

TIPS AND TRICKS

I usually set my margins to reflect the edges of my running copy. I always leave out the folios (page numbers, other text/objects that appear on each page) and objects that might bleed off the edges of the page. When it comes time to create columns for running text, PageMaker automatically uses these margins as the outside border.

To set document margins:

1. **Choose File⇨Document Setup (Figure 9).**

   The Document Setup dialog box (**Figure 10**) will appear.

   If you haven't yet created a document, choose File⇨New (Ctrl+N).

2. **In the Margins section, enter the four margin settings.**

   These settings are the distances from the edge of the page. For instance, the Top text field determines how far the top margin is from the top edge of your document.

3. **Click the OK button.**

   Your document will reflect the margin settings.

Margins are guidelines only

In addition to being able to change your guides by entering them in the Document Setup dialog box, you can override the current margin settings by just flat out ignoring them.

That's right, the margins are guidelines only, and you can choose whether or not you want to place items within their confines.

To place an object outside the margins, simply draw it or drag it there. PageMaker won't say boo about your rebelliousness.

Understanding the Cosmic Importance of Margins

To save a PageMaker document for the first time:

1. **Choose File⇨Save (Figure 11).**

   Or press Ctrl+S.

   The Save Publication dialog box will appear (**Figure 12**).

   (If you've previously saved the document, the Save command will overwrite your existing saved file, updating any changes you have made since the last time you saved.)

2. **In the Save Publication dialog box, type the name of the document you're saving.**

   Be as descriptive as possible using the standard 8.3 naming conventions. If the document will only be used on WIN95 systems, use as many characters as needed. The extension for pagemaker 6.5 documents is .P65, so a document might be named FLYER.P65.

3. **Set the location where the file should be saved.**

   By default, PageMaker will attempt to save your file in the PageMaker application directory. Don't let it do this. Instead, pick a directory (or create one) that contains other documents or nothing else.

4. **Click the Save button.**

   The document will be saved.

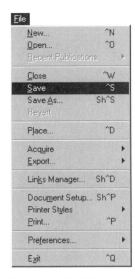

Figure 11. Choose Save from the File menu.

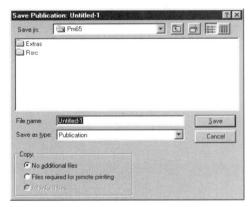

Figure 12 The Save Publication dialog box.

Save yourself time, money, and aggravation...

...By following the guidelines listed here for saving documents. Saving is undoubtedly the most important function of PageMaker, a function that I compulsively use.

After working with PageMaker for more than ten years, I've had my share of power outages, system crashes, un-undoable actions, and more. I save after writing every few paragraphs, and usually several times while designing a single page. The save process is integrated into my head so much that I've been known to do a mental Ctrl+S before turning onto a dirt road. Mental Ctrl+S's don't work, by the way.

Save frequently

Theoretically, you *can* save too much. That would be saving after each keystroke, menu selection, or mouse movement. But saving after every few keystrokes, menu selections, or mouse movements might not be that far over the top...

Here are some guidelines for determining Save points:

Before you print. Printing has always been a trouble-making procedure. To make matters worse, not only can PageMaker or your system crash when printing, but it's unlikely you'll ever see that printout after the crash.

After you've done something icky. By something icky, I mean something that you never want to do again. This may be typing a list of good times to save (heh), or it may be aligning several placed images up "just so." If you don't want to do it again, Save.

If you're walking away from your computer. Who knows what Henry in the cubicle next to you does in *your* cubicle when you visit the little boys/girls room. Maybe nothing. Maybe, however, he attempts to read your e-mail, play a quick game of Diablo, or decides that you really don't need that WIN.INI file.

If you haven't saved during the last 10 minutes. Try to save on a regular basis. It really helps.

Right after you think to yourself "I'll save right after..." No. Do it right away. Computers can read your mind and they're a vindictive lot.

Use descriptive names

Naming a file "stuff" gives it a home on your hard drive, but in a week you'll never know what "stuff" is. Be as descriptive as possible. Windows automatically appends .p65 to PageMaker 6.5 files (it used pm6 for PageMaker 6.0).

To change the name of a saved document:

1. Locate your PageMaker document on your hard drive (Figure 13).

2. Right-click on your document (Figure 14).

   Menu options for that file appear in a drop-down list.

3. Choose Rename from the list.

   The document's name will become highlighted (**Figure 15**).

4. Type in the new name for the document (Figure 16).

   If you place the cursor within the existing text, you'll add characters. If you don't click before typing, you'll replace the old name.

5. Press Enter.

   Pressing Enter after typing the name tells your computer that you're done changing the name.

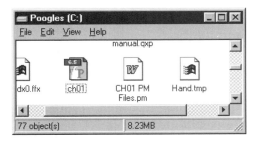

Figure 13. Locate the PageMaker document.

Figure 14. Right-click on the document.

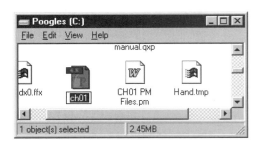

Figure 15. Choose Rename from the drop-down list and the name will be highlighted.

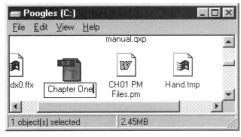

Figure 16. Type the new name of the document, then press Enter or Return.

Figure 17. Choose Save As from the File menu.

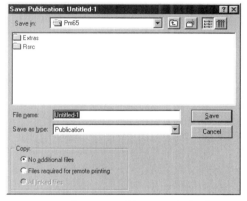

Figure 18. The Save Publication dialog box.

Figure 19. Choose Close from the File menu.

To make a duplicate document in PageMaker:

1. **With the document open in PageMaker, choose File⇨Save.**

   This saves the original document.

2. **Choose File⇨Save As (Figure 17).**

   The Save Publication dialog box (**Figure 18**) will appear.

3. **Type a different name or choose a different location for the file.**

   Either one will do.

4. **Press Enter.**

   The document is now saved and is retitled the name you've just entered in the Save Publication dialog box.

   To continue working on the original document, follow the steps below.

5. **Choose File⇨Close (Figure 19).**

   The current document is closed.

6. **Choose File⇨Open and locate the original file, then press the Open button.**

   Opening files is discussed in more detail later in this chapter.

   At this point you'll be working with the original file.

Duplicating PageMaker Documents

To revert to the last-saved version of a document:

1. **Choose File ⇨ Revert (Figure 20).**

   A dialog box will appear (**Figure 21**) asking if you really want to do this.

2. **Click the OK button.**

   The document reverts back to however it was last saved.

   This is a very powerful function and should only be done with care. You always have one Undo available for most functions, so try that first if possible.

   Remember that the Revert command takes the document to the state it was when it was last saved. If that was a ways back, you might want to consider whether it will be more work to re-create what you've done since then, or to fix what you've recently done that you to want to undo.

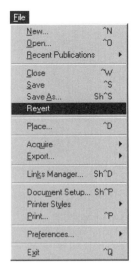

Figure 20. Choose Revert from the File menu.

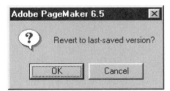

Figure 21. The Revert dialog box gives you a second chance to think about losing your most recent changes.

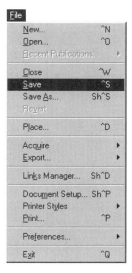

Figure 22. Choose Save from the File menu.

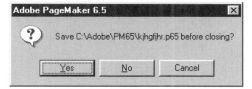

Figure 23. The Save Changes? dialog box.

Figure 24. Choose Close from the File menu.

To close a PageMaker document:

1. **Choose File ➪ Save (Figure 22).**

   Always save your changes before closing. If you don't, you'll be presented with a dialog box that asks if you'd like to save your changes anyway (**Figure 23**). But saving before closing is a good habit to get into.

2. **Choose File ➪ Close (Ctrl+W) (Figure 24).**

   The document will vanish from the screen.

TIPS AND TRICKS

Be careful when you get the Save Changes? dialog box (**Figure 24**). This dialog box lets you answer Yes, No, or Cancel. Yes updates the file on your hard drive, No leaves it alone (you lose your changes since the last Save), and Cancel returns you to your document like nothing happened. There are times when you won't want to save your changes. That's when you choose No.

Closing PageMaker Documents

To open a PageMaker document from within PageMaker:

1. Choose File⇨Open (**Figure 25**).
   Or press Ctrl+O.
   The Open Publication dialog box appears (**Figure 26**).

2. Locate the file you want to open.

3. Double-click on that file.
   The file will open in PageMaker.

To open a PageMaker document from Windows:

1. **Locate the file you want to open.**

2. **Double-click on the file.**
   The file will open in PageMaker.
   If PageMaker was not running, it will launch and open the file automatically.
   In order for PageMaker to open a file this way, the document *must* have the .p65 extension. If you'll be opening files created on a Macintosh system, be sure to either tell the person saving the files to include this extension or be aware that you'll have to rename the file before opening it.

Figure 25. Choose Open from the File menu.

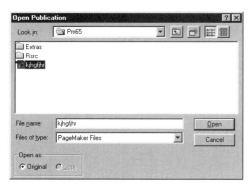

Figure 26. The Open Publication dialog box.

Multiple PageMaker documents

You can have an unlimited number of PageMaker documents open at one time. This makes transferring items between two or more documents a breeze, and it also allows you to compare or reference documents side by side.

To open a second (or third, or fourth, etc.) document in PageMaker:

1. Choose File ⇨ Open.

   Or press Ctrl+O.

   The Open Publication dialog box appears.

2. Locate the file you want to open.

3. Double-click on that file.

   The file will open in front of the already-open PageMaker document (**Figure 27**).

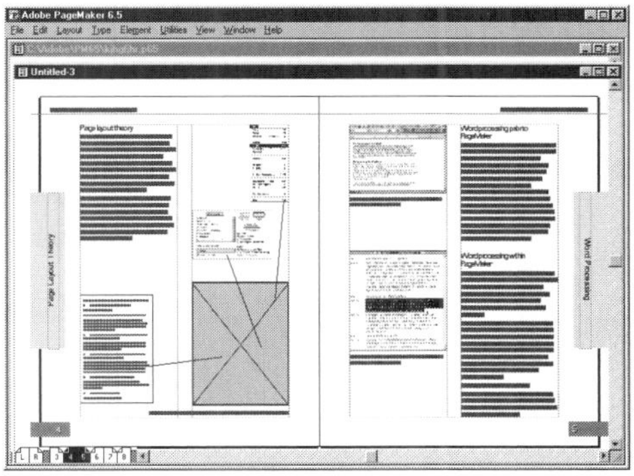

Figure 27. Two documents open in PageMaker at once, with the current document "in front" of the other document.

Opening Multiple Files

To quit PageMaker:

Choose File ⇨ Exit (Figure 28).

Or press Ctrl+Q.

If no documents are open, PageMaker will quit instantly. If one or more unsaved documents are open, a message (**Figure 29**) will appear asking if you want to save changes before closing. If you haven't made any changes to an open document, it will close automatically.

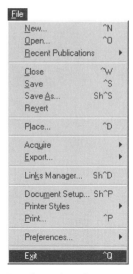

Figure 28. *Choose Exit from the File menu.*

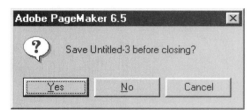

Figure 29. *The dialog box that appears when unsaved documents are open at the time of quitting.*

THE PAGEMAKER ENVIRONMENT

4

The world PageMaker lives in is populated with palettes, menus, and dialog boxes. After using PageMaker for a few months, you'll feel right at home in its world. But until then, this chapter is a guide to finding your way around without stumbling.

The areas unique to PageMaker, such as the Pasteboard and many of the palettes, are dissected throughout this chapter. In fact, this could be considered the only "reference" chapter in this book; come back to it when you need to.

The PageMaker pasteboard

The pasteboard in PageMaker is analogous to a conventional paste-up board. It is a fixed-size area that includes the document, objects that bleed off the document, and objects that lie totally outside of the document's boundaries. **Figure 1** shows a PageMaker document (one for a spread in this chapter) as it appears lying on the pasteboard.

The pasteboard is huge. **Figure 2** shows almost the entire pasteboard in one window, with the document reduced substantially. The vertical lines towards the edges of the windows are the horizontal borders of the pasteboard; no objects may exist in part or in whole outside these borders.

A conventional pasteboard was used (and undoubtedly still is, in remote jungle prepress houses and the eastern portion of Lancaster County, Pennsylvania) as a giant area where objects would be placed, and where a page or pages of a document would be set up.

Once all the elements on the pasteboard were assembled by pasting them into place (usually with a hot wax adhesive that made everything seem like a Post-It Note), the pasteboard would be carried into the camera room, placed expertly under a giant camera, and a photo would be taken of the pasteboard. The negative from the photo would be used to create printing plates (through a process called "burning"). Those plates would be attached to a printing press, and pages would be printed.

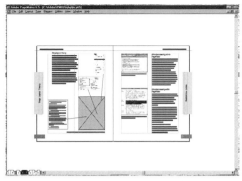

Figure 1. The PageMaker pasteboard with a document smack dab in the middle of it.

Figure 2. The same document as Figure 1, but reduced to show almost the entire pasteboard.

The big steps that PageMaker avoids are the time-consuming hand assembly of items on a page, and having to shoot negatives of the pasteboard with the camera. Instead, PageMaker can be used to create negatives instantly by printing to an imagesetter (kind of a big, ugly printer which requires you to develop the resulting film or paper via a chemical processor).

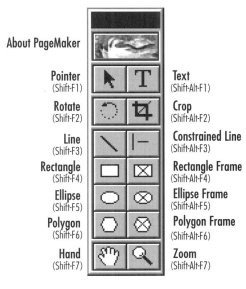

About PageMaker

Pointer (Shift-F1)	Text (Shift-Alt-F1)
Rotate (Shift-F2)	Crop (Shift-Alt-F2)
Line (Shift-F3)	Constrained Line (Shift-Alt-F3)
Rectangle (Shift-F4)	Rectangle Frame (Shift-Alt-F4)
Ellipse (Shift-F5)	Ellipse Frame (Shift-Alt-F5)
Polygon (Shift-F6)	Polygon Frame (Shift-Alt-F6)
Hand (Shift-F7)	Zoom (Shift-Alt-F7)

Figure 3. The PageMaker toolbox. Press the shortcut indicated under the name of each tool to access that tool at any time without using the mouse.

Figure 4. Choose Show Tools from the Window menu to show the toolbox.

Figure 5. Choose Hide Tools from the Window menu to hide the toolbox.

The toolbox and PageMaker's tools

The PageMaker toolbox (shown in **Figure 3**) contains all the tools that are used in PageMaker. The toolbox is normally visible, but it can be hidden and displayed through a command in the Window menu.

To show the toolbox:

Choose Window⇨Show Tools (Figure 4).

The toolbox will appear in front of your document window.

If the toolbox has been moved from its customary upper-left position before it was hidden, it will reappear where it was before it was hidden.

To hide the toolbox:

Choose Window⇨Hide Tools (Figure 5).

The toolbox will vanish from the screen.

TIPS AND TRICKS

It's easy to remember the keyboard shortcuts for accessing PageMaker tools: the left column uses Shift, the right column uses Shift-Alt. Each row increases by one, starting at F1 for the Pointer and Text tools. So the Polygon Frame tool would be Shift+Alt+F6, since it is in the right column and is the sixth tool from the top.

The PageMaker Toolbox

39

The PageMaker screen

Figure 6 shows a typical PageMaker screen, with a PageMaker document open.

In the view shown here, the document is set to the Fit in Window size, so it completely fills up the PageMaker document window.

The PageMaker Screen

Menu Bar
Most of PageMaker's commands are accessed by pull-down menus from the menu bar.

Toolbox
Tools can be selected by clicking on each tool, and then by clicking or clicking and dragging, within a document.

Master Page Icons
View master pages by clicking on either the L or R master page icons.

Document Page Icons
View a specific page in the document by clicking on the icon for that page.

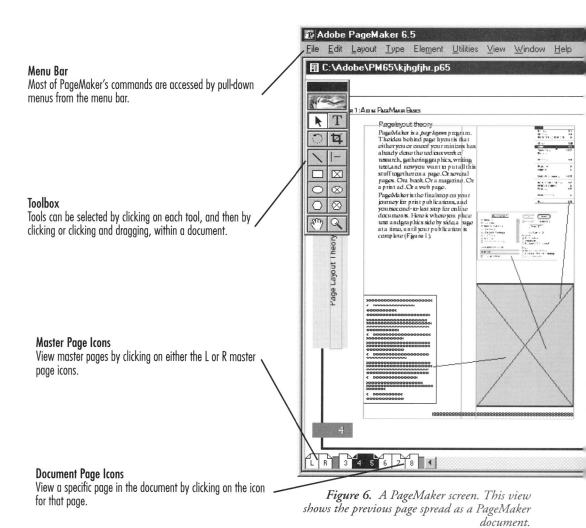

Figure 6. *A PageMaker screen. This view shows the previous page spread as a PageMaker document.*

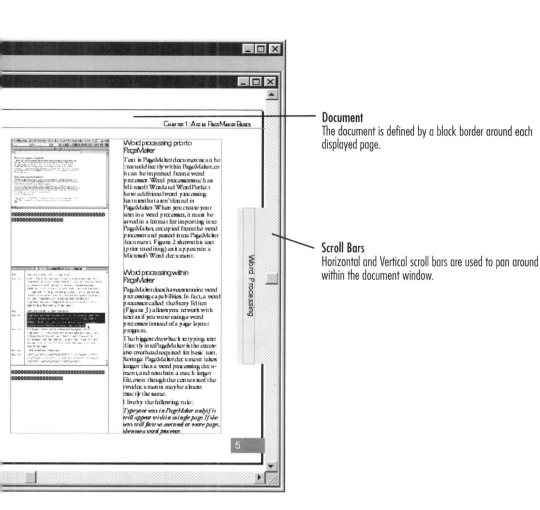

Document
The document is defined by a black border around each
displayed page.

Scroll Bars
Horizontal and Vertical scroll bars are used to pan around
within the document window.

To use menu items in PageMaker:

1. Click on the menu name in the menu bar that contains the item you wish to use (**Figure 7**).

   The menu will appear below the menu name you clicked on.

2. Move the cursor down to the menu item you want to use and click the mouse button (**Figure 8**).

   The menu action will take place (**Figure 9**). In this case, we chose Document Setup, and the Document Setup dialog box appeared.

Figure 7. *Clicking on File in the menu bar displays the File menu.*

Figure 8. *Pull down to the menu item you wish to choose, then click the mouse button.*

TIPS AND TRICKS

A slightly faster way to choose menu items is to click and hold on the left mouse button, dragging down to the menu item, and then releasing the mouse button at that point.

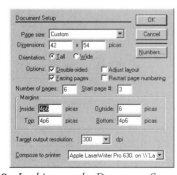

Figure 9. *In this case, the Document Setup dialog box appears after choosing Document Setup from the File menu.*

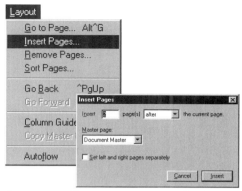

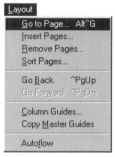

Figure 10. Choosing a menu item that has an ellipsis (...) results in a dialog box.

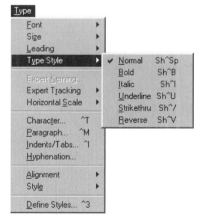

Figure 11. Menu items with keyboard commands can be accessed by pressing the appropriate keyboard command. In this case, you can activate Go to Page by pressing Ctrl+Alt+G.

Special menu items

There are a number of special ways in which menus act:

Ellipsis (...) An ellipsis following the name of a menu item means that a dialog box will appear when that menu item is chosen, as shown in **Figure 10**.

Ctrl/Shift/Alt When the symbols for Windows modifier keys are present to the right of the menu item, you can press those keys in order to access that item. For instance, you can press Ctrl+Alt+G instead of choosing Go to Page from the Layout menu (**Figure 11**).

Right Arrows If a right arrow (triangle) appears to the right of a menu item (**Figure 12**), choosing that menu item will display a submenu.

Figure 12. Submenus appear off menu items with a right arrow (triangle).

Special Menu Items

Using rulers

In addition to showing the general size and position of objects in a document, the rulers also show the exact location of your cursor, displayed as a dotted line in each ruler. The rulers display units in the current measurement system.

The ruler origin (where the ruler starts measuring from) is in the upper-left corner by default. However, you can change the origin to any location on the pasteboard, so you can measure from a different location than the upper left.

To view rulers:

Choose View⇨Show Rulers (Figure 13).

Rulers will appear along the top and left sides of the document window (Figure 14).

To hide rulers:

Choose View⇨Hide Rulers (Figure 15).

Rulers will disappear from the top and the left of the document window.

Figure 13. Show rulers by choosing Show Rulers from the View menu.

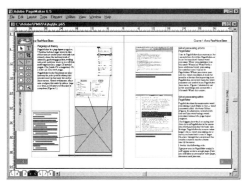

Figure 14. Rulers displayed in a document.

Figure 15. Hide rulers by choosing Hide Rulers from the View menu.

TIPS AND TRICKS

The cursor positioning markers in the rulers are handy when you are typing in a PageMaker document, as the cursor is invisible during these times.

Showing and Hiding Rulers

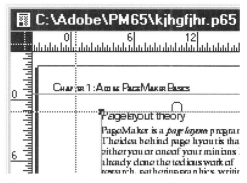

Figure 16. Click and drag from the ruler origin marker where the markers meet.

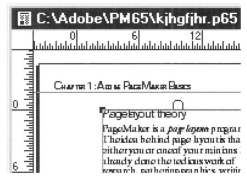

Figure 17. The ruler origin marker box changes to an empty white square when the Zero Lock option is chosen from the View menu.

To move the ruler origin:

Click and drag from the ruler origin marker (Figure 16) to a new location.

When you release the mouse button, the ruler location will be reset to the new location.

To reset the ruler origin:

Double-click on the ruler origin marker.

The ruler origin will be reset to the upper left of the document.

To lock the ruler origin:

Choose View ⇨ Zero Lock.

The ruler origin marker will change from two dotted lines to an empty white square (**Figure 17**).

Snapping to ruler increments

PageMaker provides this feature to help you align objects while dragging them. When Snap to Rulers is on, dragging any object will result in that object aligning with a ruler marker. This way no objects are a "hair" off.

To snap to ruler increments:

1. **Choose View ⇨ Snap to Rulers.**

   Ruler snapping is turned on.

2. **Drag an object and release the mouse button.**

   The object will automatically snap to a ruler marker.

There are five different measurement systems that you can use within PageMaker. There are two different ways to use different measurement systems:

Change the default. You can switch the default measurement system to any system in General Preferences.

Use a measurement suffix. By using a suffix, you can specify a different measurement system than the default one, which is handy for temporary adjustments.

To change the default measurement system:

1. **Choose File ➪ Preferences ➪ General (Figure 18).**

   The General Preferences dialog box appears (**Figure 19**).

2. **Choose an item from the Measurements in pop-up menu (Figure 20).**

   That choice will become the default measurement system.

3. **Choose a corresponding measurement from the Vertical ruler pop-up menu.**

   Usually, you'll want the vertical ruler to match the default measurement system. If you're laying out a newspaper or other publication that requires different horizontal and vertical systems (newspapers usually use picas across and inches down), adjust the menu accordingly.

Figure 18. To change the default measurement, choose General from the Preferences submenu in the File menu.

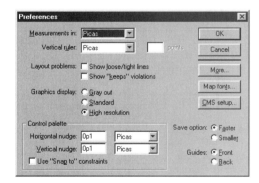

Figure 19. The General Preferences dialog box.

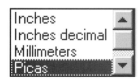

Figure 20. The Measurements in pop-up menu.

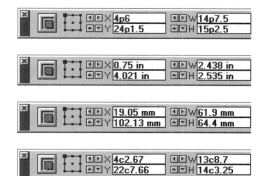

Figure 21. The Control palette with the same object selected, shown from top to bottom in picas, inches, millimeters, and ciceros.

To use a measurement system other than the one currently set in General Preferences:

In any text field where measurements are entered, use the appropriate suffix after any measurement.

For instance, placing a *p* after a number would mark that number as picas. The following list shows how each measurement system can be defined:

Inches: 1in or 1"

Inches Decimal: .1in or .1"

Picas: 1p

Picas are commonly used for typesetting measurements. There are six picas in one inch, making fractions of an inch much easier to express than by using inch-based measurements.

Points: p1 or 1 pt

There are 12 points in a pica, and 72 points in an inch. Points are used along with picas for typesetting measurements, and are used exclusively to measure type size and leading.

Millimeters: 1 mm

Ciceros: 1c

Ciceros are a European version of North America's picas. However, they aren't easily divided into any other measurement system.

Figure 21 shows the Control palette with the same item selected in several different measurements.

PageMaker's palettes all work pretty much the same way when it comes to showing and Hiding them. The following examples use the Colors palette; you can use the same steps with any other PageMaker palette.

To show the Colors palette:

Choose Window⇨Show Colors (**Figure 22**).

The Colors palette appears (**Figure 23**).

To hide the Colors palette:

Choose Window⇨Hide Colors (**Figure 24**).

The Colors palette disappears. The Colors palette can also be closed by clicking the close box (upper-right corner) of the palette.

To hide all palettes at once:

1. Make sure the Text tool is not selected in the toolbox. If it is, either click on another tool or press Ctrl-Space to switch to the Pointer tool.

   The feature that hides all palettes doesn't work with the Text tool because the Tab key is used; when typing text, the Tab key inserts a tab.

2. Press the Tab key.

   All palettes (including the toolbox) will disappear. Press Tab again to show the hidden palettes.

Figure 22. Choose Show Colors from the Window menu to display the Colors palette.

Figure 23. The Colors palette.

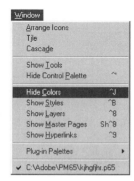

Figure 24. Choose Hide Colors from the Window menu to hide the Colors palette.

Showing and Hiding Palettes

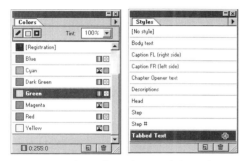

Figure 25. The Styles palette and the Colors palette shown as individual palettes.

Figure 26. The combined palettes.

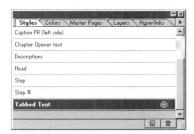

Figure 27. All of PageMaker's embeddable palettes in one palette shell.

PageMaker's palettes can be combined into a single palette shell with different palettes accessible by clicking on their respective tabs.

To combine palettes:

1. Display all the palettes you want to combine on the screen (**Figure 25**).

2. Drag a palette *into* another palette and release the mouse button.

   You can tell a palette will be placed within another palette when the target palette gets a dark border around it.

   When you release the mouse button, the two palettes will be in one "shell" with tabs showing which palette is active (**Figure 26**).

To make an embedded palette active:

Click on its tab within the palette shell.

The white tab is always the active one.

TIPS AND TRICKS

You can combine every one of PageMaker's palettes into a single shell (**Figure 27**). This dramatically reduces the amount of space used by palettes.

Combining Palettes

PageMaker's palettes

These pages provide a handy reference for each of PageMaker's palettes, with each palette's pop-up menu shown. The workings of each palette are discussed in different chapters throughout this book.

The Colors palette

The Colors palette (**Figure 28**) is used to apply colors to objects and text. Press Ctrl+J to show and hide the palette. The Colors palette is discussed in Chapter 14: Coloring.

The Styles palette

The Styles palette (**Figure 29**) is used to apply Paragraph styles (font, point size, leading, alignment, tabs, and more) to text. Press Ctrl+B to show and hide the Styles palette. The Styles palette is discussed in Chapter 9: Styles.

The Layers palette

The Layers palette (**Figure 30**) is used to organize your document elements (text and graphical objects) into layers which can be independently viewed and locked. Press Ctrl+8 to show and hide the Layers palette. The Layers palette is discussed in Chapter 17: Layers.

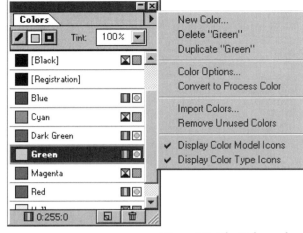

Figure 28. The Colors palette.

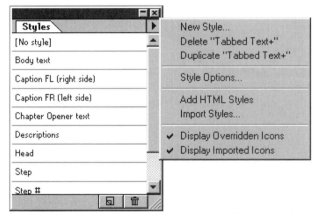

Figure 29. The Styles palette.

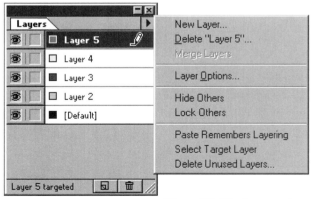

Figure 30. The Layers palette.

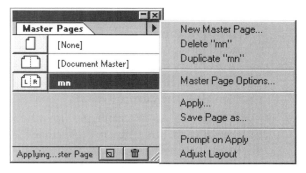

Figure 31. The Master Pages palette.

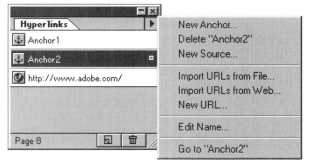

Figure 32. The Hyperlinks palette.

Figure 33. The Control palette.

The Master Pages palette

The Master Pages palette (**Figure 31**) is used to create, modify, and apply multiple master pages to pages within a PageMaker document. Press Ctrl+Alt+8 to show and hide the palette. The Master Pages palette is discussed in Chapter 19: Master Pages.

The Hyperlinks palette

The Hyperlinks palette (**Figure 32**) is used to attach links to any PageMaker element. Press Ctrl+9 to show and hide the Hyperlinks palette. The Hyperlinks palette is discussed in Chapter 21: Web Pages.

The Control palette

The Control palette (**Figure 33**) is used to move and adjust graphical and text elements. The palette changes appearance based on the selected objects. The version shown at the top appears when graphical objects are selected. The bottom version displays when text is selected with the Text tool. Press Ctrl+' to show and hide the palette. The Control palette is discussed in Chapters 7, 8, and 11.

PageMaker's Palettes

Math in PageMaker Text Fields

Performing mathematical operations in PageMaker's Text Fields

PageMaker's number-based text fields (any place in a palette or dialog box where you can enter numerical text) allow you to perform several basic mathematical operations. To make type six points larger, you can type a **+6** after the current value. To make type ten points smaller, you can type a **-10** after the current value.

While that's just fine for those of us who can't take off our socks because we're in an office environment, PageMaker goes a few steps further.

In measurement and size text fields, you can use multiple measurement types. For instance, if your measurement system is picas, you can add and subtract in inches or millimeters. As long as you indicate the measurement system within PageMaker (see page 47), you can mix and match as many systems as you'd like. For instance, to move an element currently located at 3p across two inches to the right, you would enter **3p+2in** in the text field (you only have to type the **+2in** if you click your cursor to the right of the 3p; if you highlight the entire text field, you'll have to type the full amount).

But that's not all. You can also do multiplication and division within text fields. Want to make something a third of its size? Just enter **/3** after the value. To multiply by three, enter ***3** after the current value.

If you want to use multiple operands (more than one plus, minus, divide or multiply) in a text field, you can. The math will follow the same rules traditional math does: left to right, multiplication and division before addition and subtraction.

You can change the order of the math by using parentheses around certain operands, such as **(6+2)*3** instead of **6+2*3**. The result of the first equation would be 24 (6+2=8, and 8 times 3 equals 24), while the result of the second equation would be 12 (2 times 3 equals 6, and 6+6=12).

If all this confuses you, hunt down a fourth grade math book (that's what I did) which makes all this silly math stuff much clearer.

P | TIPS AND TRICKS

Certain text fields only accept specific measurement systems. For instance, the type size text field only accepts points, not picas, inches, or millimeters.

Figure 34. The View menu.

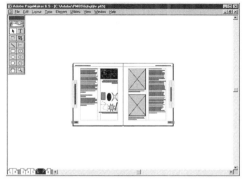

Figure 35. A document viewed at 25% of its actual size.

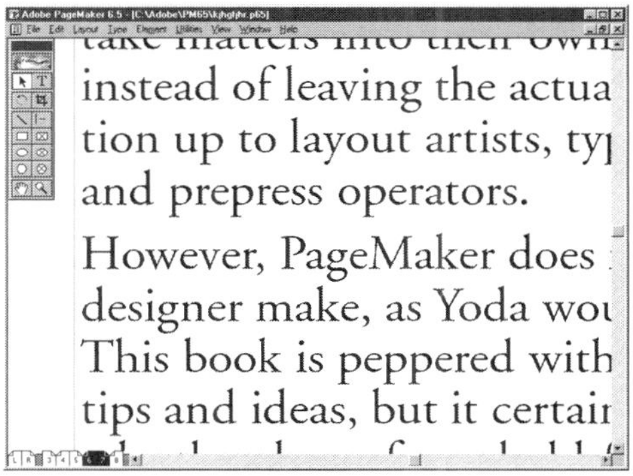

PageMaker's Viewing Options

PageMaker's View menu (**Figure 34**) provides all sorts of ways to customize the way you work with PageMaker documents. In addition, the Hand tool and Zoom tool provide quick methods for panning and zooming within your document.

PageMaker lets you view documents at multiple magnifications, from 25% to 400%. Viewing the document at a different magnification doesn't change the document itself, it only changes the way you see it. While your text and images will look absolutely huge on screen when you're viewing your document at 400%, the text and images haven't really changed in size. They will print the same regardless of your magnification setting. To make text and images larger or smaller, you'll need to scale them using the Control palette or through the appropriate dialog box.

Figure 35 shows a document window with the magnification set to 25%. **Figure 36** shows the same document at 400%. The level of detail changes on screen, but the document itself has not changed.

*Figure 36. The document from **Figure 35** at 400% of actual size.*

Viewing Options

The most useful way to view a document is the Actual Size setting, which attempts to show you, on screen, the exact physical size of your document.

To view a document at Actual Size:

Choose View ⇨ Actual Size (Ctrl+1) (Figure 37).

or

Double-click on the Zoom tool in the toolbox (Figure 38).

Either method will redraw your document at 100%, meaning that on a screen with a resolution of 72 ppi, your document is precisely the same size on screen as when you print it.

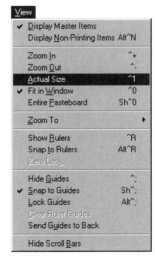

Figure 37. Choose Actual Size from the View menu to view your document at 100%, which should approximate the size of the document when printed.

TIPS AND TRICKS

Since the advent of Multisync monitors a few years ago, Actual Size and 100% are less and less accurate. If your monitor's resolution is set to 72 ppi, it should be fairly accurate. However, if you use a higher resolution (like 1024 x 768 on a 14" monitor), "actual size" will be displayed much smaller on screen than the page really is. Likewise, if you lower the resolution (such as 640 x 480 on a 21" monitor), the document will appear much larger on screen than it will print.

Figure 38. Double-click on the Zoom tool (the magnifying glass) in the toolbox to quickly change to Actual Size view.

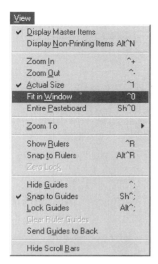

Figure 39. Choose Fit in Window from the View menu to reduce the document so that either one page or an entire spread can be seen in its entirety within the document window.

To change to Fit in Window view:

Choose View⇨Fit in Window (**Ctrl+0**) (**Figure 39**).

or

Double-click on the Hand tool in the toolbox.

Doing either will do two things. First, one page (or a spread if left and right pages are active) will be resized so that the entire document fits within the current window size. Second, the document is positioned so that it *is* entirely within the document window (**Figure 40**).

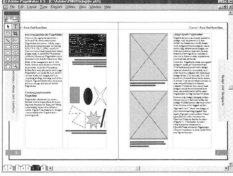

Figure 40. A document shown in Fit in Window mode.

TIPS AND TRICKS

These viewing options (in addition to fonts and graphics displaying on the screen) are where the ugly 80's acronym/phrase WYSIWYG (pronounced "wizzywig"), which stands for What You See Is What You Get, came from. Of course, in the mid-eighties when scanners were a luxury few could afford, and typefaces looked horrendous above 24 points, it was much more like WYSISLWYEGIYGIAA (pronounced "wizzizilwieguyguya") meaning, What You See Is Somewhat Like What You'll Eventually Get, If You Get It At All.

You can zoom in and out of your PageMaker document by using the Zoom tool. The Zoom tool allows you to zoom either one step at a time, or to quickly zoom into a specific area.

To zoom in one step at a time:

1. Choose the Zoom tool from the toolbox or press and hold Ctrl+Space to access it temporarily.

2. Click on the area you wish to zoom into.

    That area will be enlarged. **Figure 41** shows a document before zooming in, and **Figure 42** shows that same document after zooming in.

    Continue clicking to keep zooming in.

To zoom out one step at a time:

1. Choose the Zoom tool from the toolbox or press and hold Ctrl+Space to access it temporarily.

2. Alt+Click on the document.

    That area will be reduced.

To Zoom in on a specific area:

Using the Zoom tool, drag around the area you wish to zoom in to (Figure 43).

That area will fill the document window.

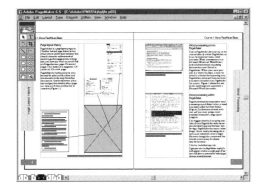

Figure 41. The document prior to zooming in.

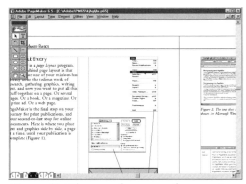

Figure 42. The same document after zooming.

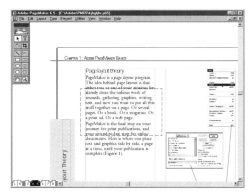

Figure 43. Drawing a marquee with the Zoom tool. The document will resize to show just the area within the marquee, blown up to fill the document window.

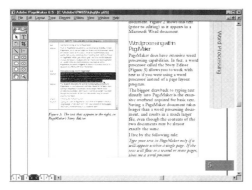

Figure 44. The document prior to panning.

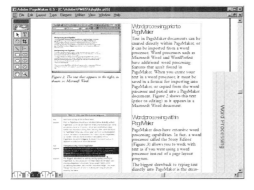

Figure 45. After panning in on the document, the top of the work area is visible.

Once you've zoomed in to a document enough, it becomes difficult to scroll around with just the scroll bars. A better way to navigate in a zoomed-in document is by panning.

To pan around a PageMaker document:

1. **Choose the Hand tool from the toolbox, or press and hold the Alt key to access the Hand tool temporarily.**

2. **Click and drag within the document.**

   As you drag, the document will move around the screen. **Figure 44** shows the document before panning, and **Figure 45** shows it after panning.

Panning

5

PageMaker allows you to adjust all sorts of features within the program, from how the program works to what default settings are used by new documents.

This flexibility is provided so that you can customize PageMaker to work the best way for you, fitting your style as you're creating publications.

Introduction to Preferences

Setting preferences for new and existing documents

When you make changes to PageMaker's preferences, you can affect either one document or any new documents yet to be created.

PageMaker knows whether you're affecting one document or future ones if you have any documents open. If you do, then the frontmost (active) document is the one that will be affected by the preference changes (the other open documents are not affected at all). If there are no open documents, then every *new* document you create will be affected by the preference changes.

Documents you *open* after you make preference changes (regardless of whether any documents were open at the time of the change or not) are *not* affected by changes you make to preferences.

Sadly, there is no way to make preference changes to more than one existing document at a time. For instance, if I wanted to change each of the chapters in this book to inches instead of picas, I would have to open each document and individually change my preferences for each one.

Beyond preferences

Besides General Preferences, there are many changes you can make that will affect new documents yet to be created. With no documents open, any changes you make will affect future documents, even if those changes aren't in the Preferences submenu.

How do you know which settings can be changed for future documents? Close all open documents, and check to see which menu items can be selected (those not grayed out) in each menu.

Here's a list of elements that can be changed when no documents are open:

The Acquire source

Document Setup

Printer Styles

All Preferences

Column Guides and Autoflow on/off

Most type options

Element changes to fill and stroke

Text Wrap options for new elements

Polygon settings

Rounded corner settings

Link options

Define Colors

Viewable items (in the View menu)

Various plug-ins

To affect future new documents, make changes to any of the above items when no documents are open. All new documents you create will incorporate the changes you've made.

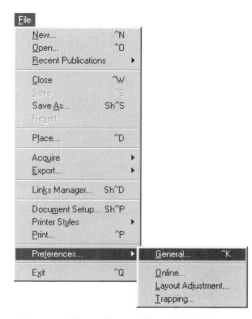

Figure 1. Choose General from the Preferences submenu in the File menu to access General Preferences.

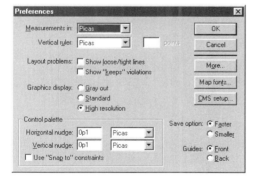

Figure 2. The Preferences dialog box.

To change preferences for a specific document:

1. **Open the document to which you wish to make preference changes.**

   The document must be open and active (i.e., in front of all other open documents) in order to change the preferences for that document.

2. **Choose File ⇨Preferences ⇨ General (Ctrl+K) (Figure 1).**

   The Preferences dialog box will appear (**Figure 2**). This is where you can make most changes to the way PageMaker works with your current document.

3. **After you've made changes in the Preferences dialog box, click OK.**

   The new changes take effect immediately.

To change preferences for all future new documents:

1. **Close all open documents.**

   If a document is open, only that document's preferences will be affected.

2. **Choose File ⇨Preferences ⇨ General (Ctrl+K).**

3. **After you've made changes in the Preferences dialog box, click OK.**

   The new changes will take effect in each new document you create.

Using the Preferences Dialog Box

The Preferences Dialog Box

Main Measurements
This sets the main measurements (what most unit measurements will appear in) for your document.

Vertical Ruler
Newspapers and other publications sometimes need to measure vertical measurements with a different system than the main measurement system.

Layout Problems
Use these checkboxes to view problems that occur when using justified type.

Graphics Display
These three options control the way that graphics are displayed on screen in PageMaker documents.

Horizontal/Vertical Nudges
When using the Control palette's nudge arrows, these settings define the amount of change that will occur when each button is pressed.

Use Snap To Constraints
This option provides automatic nudging to ruler units and guides.

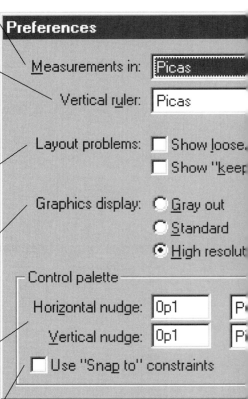

Figure 3. The Preferences dialog box.

Custom Value
If Custom is chosen from the Vertical ruler pop-up menu, you can define the custom increments by entering a point value here.

OK Button
Clicking this button (or pressing the Return or Enter keys) will put these preferences into effect.

Cancel Button
Clicking the Cancel button (or pressing the ESC key) will exit the Preferences box without making any changes.

More Button
This button displays additional preferences (see the following page).

Map Fonts
This button displays the Map fonts dialog box.

CMS Setup
This button displays the Color Management System dialog box.

Save Options
Faster enables quick incremental saves, but the file size can be quite large. Smaller is slower, but conserves disk space.

Guides
This option determines whether guides are in front of items (making them easier to select) or behind items.

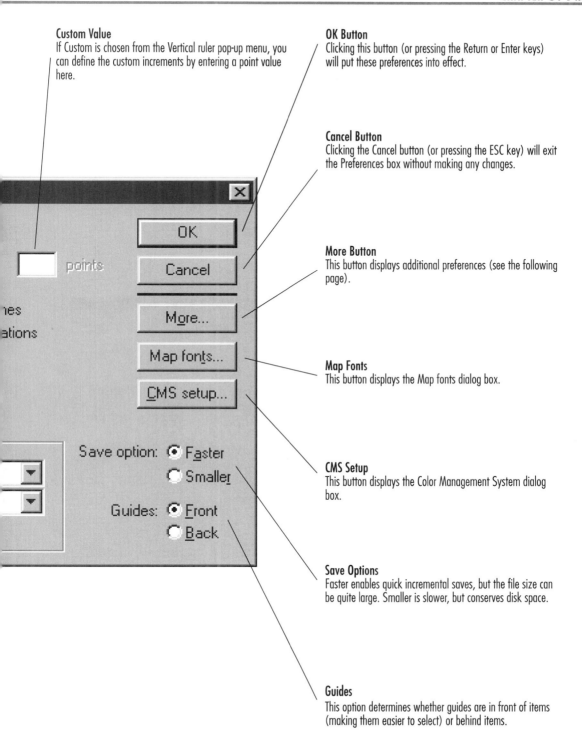

The Preferences Dialog Box

63

Greek Text Below
This value determines at what point size text is greeked (displayed as a gray box).

Turn Pages When Autoflowing
If the Autoflowing option (Layout menu) is checked, this control determines whether you view pages being turned during autoflow or not.

Use Typographer's Quotes
This option, when checked, substitutes "real" quotes instead of "inch marks."

TrueType Display
This setting determines how TrueType fonts are displayed (a similar setting is accessible in the ATM control panel for PostScript fonts).

Story Editor Options
These options control how text appears when displayed in Story Editor (Edit ➪ Edit Story) mode.

Graphics Size Controls
These settings control how the standard display is defined and if you should be alerted when an image you're embedding is larger than a certain size.

PostScript Printing
This option (set to either Normal or Maximum) allows you to define how much memory within PageMaker should be allocated to printing PostScript graphics.

To access the More Preferences dialog box:

1. **Choose File ➪ Preferences ➪ General (Ctrl+K).**
   The Preferences dialog box appears.

2. **In the Preferences dialog box, click the More button.**
   The More Preferences dialog box (**Figure 4**) will appear.

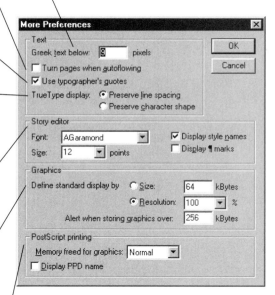

Figure 4. *The More Preferences dialog box.*

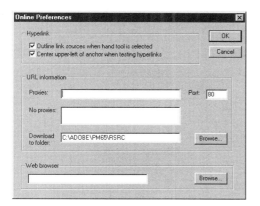

Figure 5. The Online Preferences dialog box (Chapter 21).

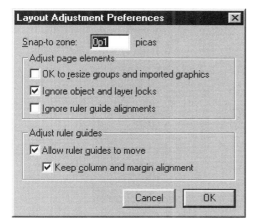

Figure 6. The Layout Adjustment Preferences dialog box (Chapter 16).

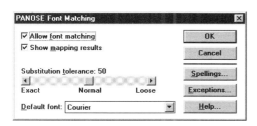

Figure 7. The Font Matching Preferences dialog box (Chapter 6).

Other Preferences

There are several other preferences in PageMaker, but each of them is discussed fully in other chapters that focus on those specific topics. **Figures 5–9** show a few of the other preference dialog boxes and the chapters in which they appear.

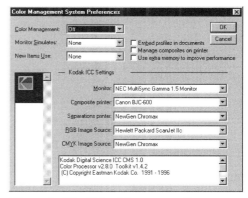

Figure 8. The Color Management System Preferences dialog box (Chapter 14).

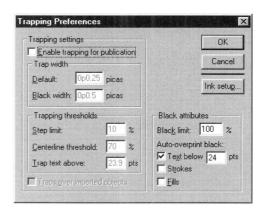

Figure 9. The Trapping Preferences dialog box (Chapter 23).

Other Preferences

TYPE

One of PageMaker's greatest strengths is its ability to edit and manipulate type. This is accomplished through the use of text blocks (which are often called windowshades) and the text that resides within those text blocks.

The Text tool

PageMaker's Text tool is used for three primary purposes:

- **Creating new text areas.**

  Text in PageMaker must exist inside a text block (or a frame being used as a text block), and the Text tool is used to create those text blocks.

- **Selecting text.**

  In order to make changes to existing text, that text must be selected with the Text tool.

- **Moving the text insertion point.**

  The little blinking insertion point can be moved by clicking at the desired location within a text block (next to any character).

To access the Text tool:

Click on the Text tool (Figure 1) in the toolbox.

You can also access the Text tool by pressing Shift+Alt+F1 on your keyboard.

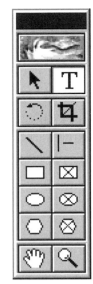

Figure 1. *Click on the Text tool in the toolbox to access it.*

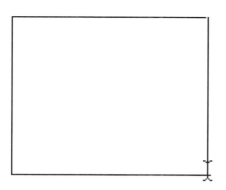

Figure 2. Drag with the Text tool to create a text block.

Figure 3. The blinking cursor appears when you release the mouse button after drawing a text block.

"some text"|

Figure 4. Be sure to type some text (any text will do, I'm just being a little literal here) after the text block is drawn.

"some text"

Figure 5. Clicking on the text block with the Pointer tool displays the text block's boundaries.

Text blocks

Text blocks are created so that text can be flowed into PageMaker. The containers are often referred to as "windowshades," because the bottom of each text block can be raised and lowered just like shades on a window.

To create a text block:

1. **Click on the Text tool.**

2. **Click and drag diagonally to draw a text block (Figure 2).**

   As you drag, you'll see a rectangle appear. This represents the boundaries of the text block.

3. **Release the mouse button (Figure 3).**

   When you release the mouse button, a blinking cursor will appear.

4. **Enter some text (Figure 4).**

   You *must* enter text at this point. If you click somewhere else or change tools, the text block you drew will vanish. PageMaker automatically deletes empty text blocks.

To view the boundaries of the text block:

1. **Select the Pointer tool.**

2. **Click on the text you just typed. (Figure 5).**

Creating Text Blocks

To change the width of a text block:

1. Choose the Pointer tool.

2. Click either the left or right handles on the bottom of the text block, and drag diagonally (**Figure 6**).

   When you release the mouse button, the text in the text block will reflow automatically to fit the shape of the text block. (**Figure 7**).

   If a red downward-pointing triangle appears (**Figure 8**), it means that you've made the text box too small for the amount of text in the current box. The text is still there, but is hidden by the bottom windowshade. Pulling the windowshade down as far as possible should show the remainder of the text. In some cases, you'll need to either make the text block wider or link it to another text block (see the next page).

   You can change the height of a text block by dragging the bottom windowshade up or down. However, if there isn't enough text to make a taller windowshade, the bottom windowshade will snap back up to the last line in the text block.

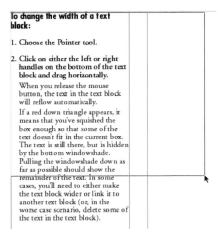

Figure 6. Drag one of the text block's lower handles and drag.

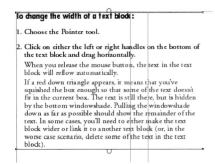

Figure 7. When you release the mouse button, the text reflows into the new shape.

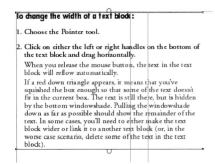

Figure 8. If you make the text block too small for the text to fit into it, a red downward triangle appears at the bottom of the text block.

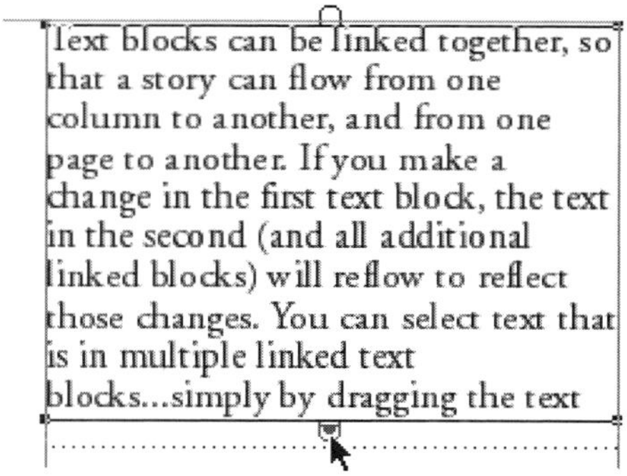

Text blocks can be linked together, so that a story can flow from one column to another, and from one page to another. If you make a change in the first text block, the text in the second (and all additional linked blocks) will reflow to reflect those changes. You can select text that is in multiple linked text blocks...simply by dragging the text

Figure 9. Pull the bottom of the windowshade up until a red triangle appears.

Figure 10. After clicking the triangle, the cursor will change into this shape, indicating that you are "carrying" text.

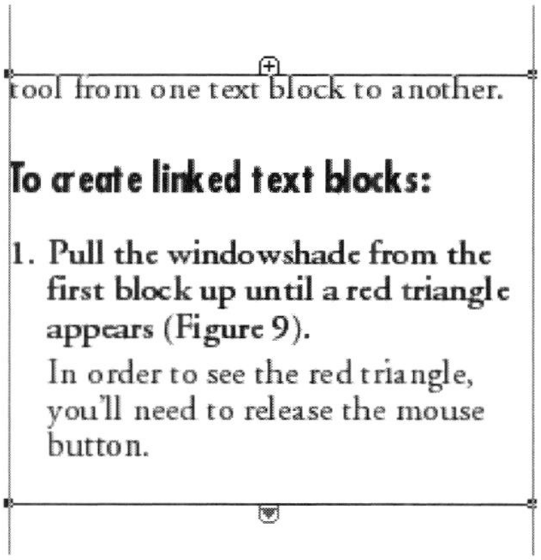

tool from one text block to another.

To create linked text blocks:

1. Pull the windowshade from the first block up until a red triangle appears (Figure 9).

   In order to see the red triangle, you'll need to release the mouse button.

Figure 11. After clicking and dragging with the cursor to create a new text block, the missing text appears when you release the mouse button.

Text blocks can be linked together, so that a story can flow from one column to another, and from one page to another. If you make a change in the first text block, the text in the second (and all subsequent linked blocks) will reflow to reflect that change. You can select text in multiple linked text blocks simply by dragging the Text tool from one text block to another.

To create linked text blocks:

1. **Pull up the windowshade from the first block until a red triangle appears (Figure 9).**

   In order to see the red triangle, you'll need to release the mouse button.

2. **Click the red triangle on the windowshade.**

   Your cursor will change into something resembling the upper-left corner of a document page (**Figure 10**).

3. **Click and drag anywhere else in your document to create the linked text block.**

   When you release the mouse button, the text will reflow into the area you dragged (**Figure 11**).

   You can create additional linked text blocks by repeating steps 1 through 3 for each new linked text block you wish to create.

Connecting Text Blocks

To automatically connect several text blocks:

1. Choose Layout ⇨ Autoflow (Figure 12).

2. Pull up the windowshade from the first block until a red triangle appears.

3. Click the red triangle on the windowshade.

   Your cursor will change into a page corner containing a squiggly arrow (**Figure 13**).

4. Click (**don't drag**) anywhere else in your document to create a series of linked text blocks.

   When you release the mouse button, the text will reflow into the column you clicked and any additional columns it needs (**Figure 14**).

   If your document doesn't have enough pages, they will be created automatically, as needed.

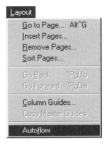

Figure 12. Choose Autoflow from the Layout menu.

Figure 13. The Autoflow cursor.

Figure 14. After automatically autoflowing into two columns.

TIPS AND TRICKS

You can quickly toggle between the Autoflow cursor and the regular Link cursor by pressing the Ctrl key.

Figure 15. Choose Place from the File menu.

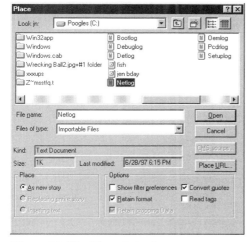

Figure 16. The Place dialog box.

Figure 17. The text carrying cursor.

make up for the 2.5 hours spent in the theater watching most of the movie. Nor does a refund. Very little does, unfortunately. We now have to either (1) go see the movie again just to catch the last 10 minutes or (2) wait until it comes to video, HBO, etc. in order to view the ending, neither prospect being particularly satisfying.

Figure 18. Text that has stopped flowing because it has reached the end of a column.

Placing text

PageMaker allows you to bring text that has been created in other software, such as a word processing program, into any PageMaker document. When you bring text into PageMaker this way, you are "Placing text."

To place text into a PageMaker document:

1. **Choose File ➪ Place (Ctrl+D) (Figure 15).**

   The Place dialog box will appear **(Figure 16)**.

2. **Locate the document that contains the text you wish to place, select it, and click the OK button.**

   The cursor will change into the text carrying shape **(Figure 17)**.

3. **Click in any column in your document to place the text.**

   If you have Autoflow turned on in the Layout menu, the text will flow into as many columns as necessary, adding pages as needed.

   If you don't have Autoflow turned on, the text will stop flowing at the bottom of the column in which you clicked **(Figure 18)**.

You can also click and drag to make the text fit into a specific text block of your design. If the text is too short for the block you've drawn, the block will automatically adjust to the proper height. If the text is too long, the text block will increase in height until it reaches the bottom of the current document page.

Whenever you import text, you'll be given the chance to modify the filter options that are used to bring in the text. Filter options are certain options that are specific to the type of document you'll be importing. Most of the time you can ignore these, but there are a few things that you might want to change now and again.

To change import filter preferences:

1. Choose File ⇨ Place (Ctrl+D).

2. Check the Show filter preferences checkbox in the Place dialog box (Figure 19).

3. Locate the document that contains the text you wish to place, select it, and click the OK button.

4. The Filter Preferences dialog box will appear for the file you selected (Figure 20).

   This example shows the Microsoft Word filter preferences. Other text formats will vary slightly.

5. Make any changes and click the OK button.

   The placed text will contain all the changes you made to the Filter Preferences dialog box.

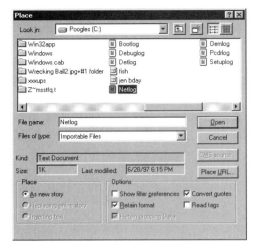

Figure 19. Check the Show filter preferences checkbox in the Place dialog box.

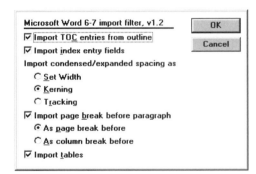

Figure 20. The Filter Preferences dialog box for Microsoft Word documents.

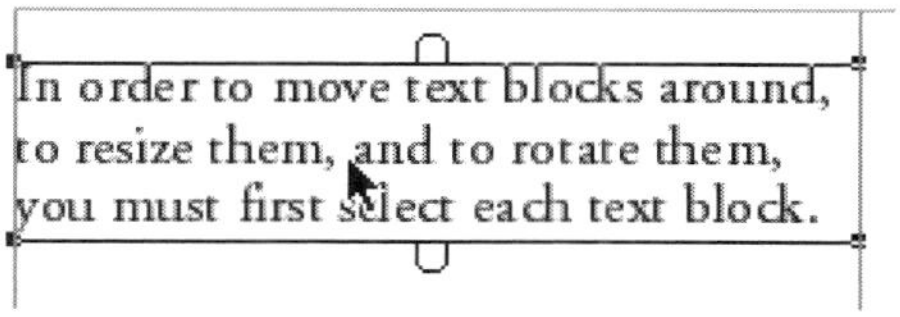

Figure 21. Click on a text block with the Pointer tool to select it.

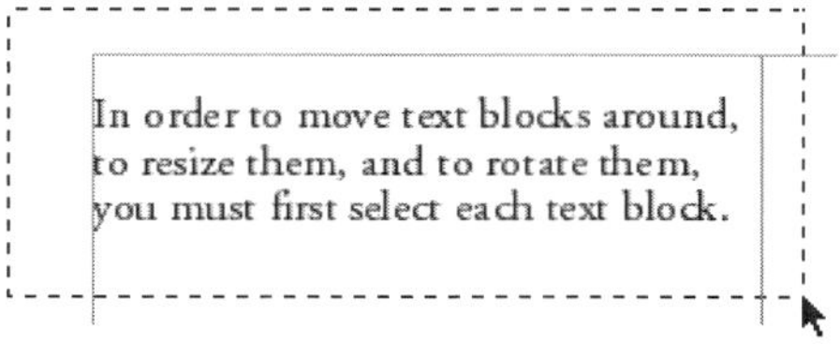

Figure 22. Drag a marquee around a text block to select it.

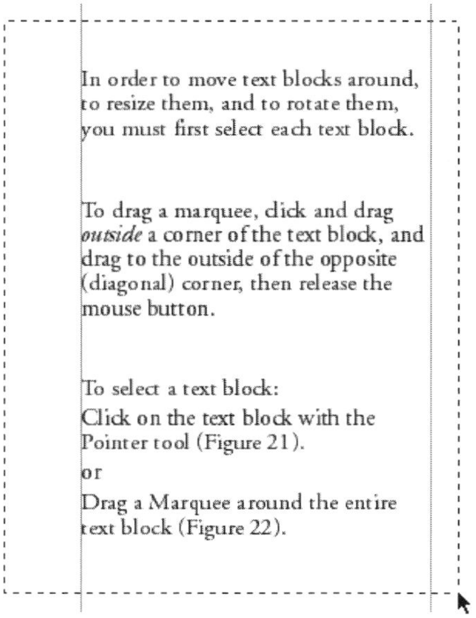

Figure 23. Drag a marquee around several text blocks to select them all at once.

In order to move text blocks around, resize them, and rotate them, you must first select each text block.

To select a text block:

Click on the text block with the Pointer tool (Figure 21).

or

Drag a Marquee around the entire text block (Figure 22).

To drag a marquee, click and drag from *outside* a corner of the text block, and drag to the outside of the opposite (diagonal) corner, then release the mouse button.

To select more than one text block:

After selecting the first text block, Shift-click on all successive text blocks.

or

Drag a marquee around several text blocks (Figure 23).

The marquee must completely encompass all the text blocks you wish to select.

To deselect selected text blocks:

With the Pointer tool, click in a blank area of your document.

or

Choose Edit ⇨ Deselect All (Ctrl+Shift+A).

Selecting Text Blocks

To move a text block:

1. **Using the Pointer tool, click on the text block and drag it.**

   You'll see the text block's outline move with your cursor as you drag (**Figure 24**).

2. **Release the mouse button.**

   The text block appears in the new location (which had been indicated by the dragged outline).

To move several text blocks at once:

1. **Select the text blocks you wish to move (using the method described on the previous page).**

2. **Click on any of the selected text blocks and drag.**

   A single, "all encompassing" outline will appear as you drag, indicating the top, bottom, left, and right of the selected text blocks.

3. **Release the mouse button.**

   The text blocks appear in the new location.

To delete one or more text blocks:

1. **Select the text block(s) to be deleted.**

2. **Press the Backspace key on your keyboard.**

   All selected text blocks will be deleted (**Figure 25**).

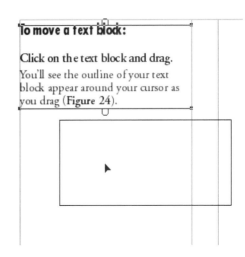

To move a text block:

Click on the text block and drag.

You'll see the outline of your text block appear around your cursor as you drag (Figure 24).

Figure 24. Click on a text block and drag with the Pointer tool. When you release the mouse button, the text block will appear in the location you dragged it to.

Figure 25. A deleted text block, as it appears on your screen...use your imagination here.

TIPS AND TRICKS

Quickly delete all the text blocks on one page by pressing Ctrl+A, then the Backspace key, when any tool but the Text tool is active. Be aware, however, that if there are graphics or picture element boxes on the same page, they will be selected and deleted as well. As with most other PageMaker activities, you can undo the deletion, but only if you choose Edit ⇨ Undo right after you've deleted the objects.

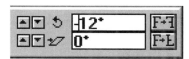

Figure 26. The rotation portion of the Control palette provides a quick method for rotating selected text blocks.

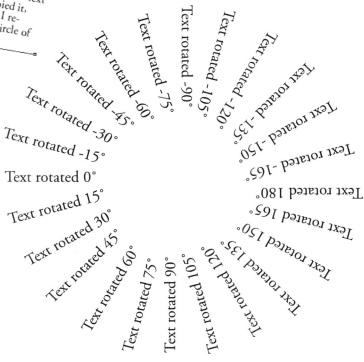

Figure 27. A text block after being rotated 10°.

To rotate a text block:

1. With the Pointer tool, select the text block you wish to rotate.

2. In the Control palette, change the rotation angle to the angle you wish to rotate the text box (Figure 26).

3. Press the Enter key.

   The text will be rotated to the degree you specified (**Figure 27**).

Common rotation appearances:

To create the chart below, I created one text block ("Text rotated 0°"), copied it, pasted it, and rotated it 15°. I repeated the process until the circle of text rotations was complete.

79

Didn't we cover text selection a few pages ago? Well, on page 77, I explained how to select text "blocks," which are the containers for text. Selecting text blocks allows you to manipulate the block's size, shape, angle, and location, and lets you delete it (and the text within it). But if you want to add text, modify the font, or do any other number of things to the text within the text block, you'll have to select the text itself.

One limitation of selecting text in PageMaker is that you can't select text in two different locations, or in two different stories (text which flows through linked text blocks). The text you select must always be *contiguous,* meaning there can be no unselected characters between selected ones.

To select one character at a time:

With the Text tool, click before the character you want to select and drag to the right until the character(s) is selected (Figure 28).

The further you drag, the more characters will be selected.

To select a word at a time:

With the Text tool, double-click on the first word you want to select (Figure 29).

If you double-click and drag, you'll select a word at a time.

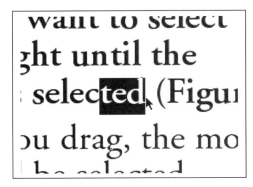

Figure 28. Click and drag with the Text tool to select one (or more) character at a time.

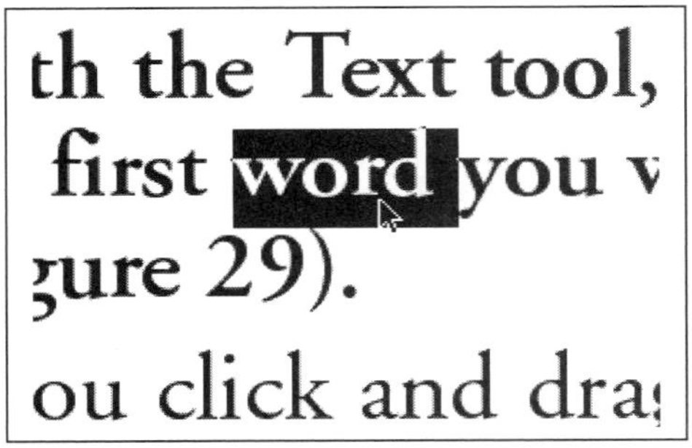

Figure 29. Double-click to select an entire word.

P TIPS AND TRICKS

When you double-click on a word with the Text tool, you select the space after that word as well. If you delete text selected in this way, the space is also deleted, avoiding the potential problem of double spaces between words. If you drag after double-clicking, the space after the last word selected will always be selected, too.

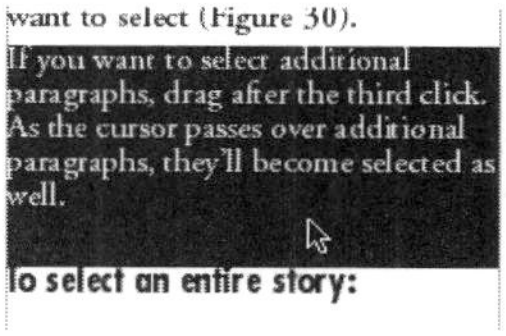

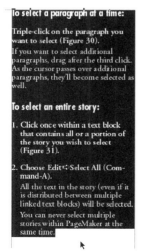

Figure 30. Triple-click to select an entire paragraph.

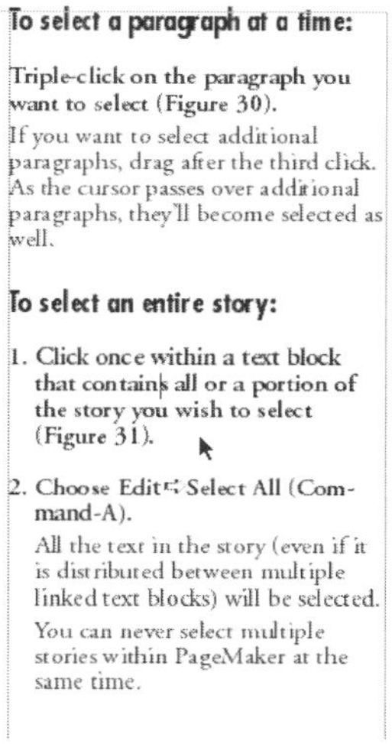

Figure 31. Click once in a text block of the story you wish to select.

Figure 32. Choose Select All to select all the text in the story.

To select a paragraph at a time:

Triple-click on the paragraph you want to select (Figure 30).

If you want to select additional paragraphs, drag after the third click. As the cursor passes over additional paragraphs, they'll become selected as well.

To select an entire story:

1. **Click once within a text block that contains all or a portion of the story you wish to select (Figure 31).**

2. **Choose Edit ⇨ Select All (Ctrl+A).**

   All text in the story (even if it is distributed between multiple linked text blocks) will be selected (**Figure 32**).

   You can never select multiple stories within PageMaker at the same time.

Selecting Text Paragraphs and Stories

81

Exporting

You can take text *out* of PageMaker, so it can be used in other applications. Text is commonly exported as a file format that you can open with a word processor.

To export text:

1. **Select the text you wish to export (Figure 33).**

   If you want to export an entire story, you can click anywhere within one of the text blocks (there's no need to select anything).

2. **Choose File ➪ Export ➪ Text (Figure 34).**

   The Export Document dialog box appears (**Figure 35**).

3. **Enter a name for the text file you're exporting.**

4. **Choose the file format from the list of formats.**

5. **If you want to export the entire story, choose that option, otherwise leave the Selected text only option selected.**

6. **Click the Save button.**

   The text will be exported to a file.

Figure 33. Select the text you wish to export.

Figure 34. Choose Text from the Export submenu of the File menu.

Figure 35. The Export Document dialog box.

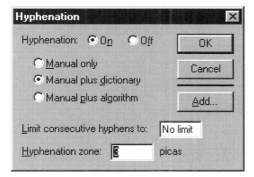

Figure 36. Choose Hyphenation from the Type menu.

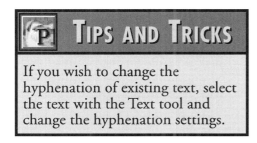

Figure 37. The Hyphenation dialog box.

To turn on hyphenation:

There are two ways to activate hyphenation.

1. **Choose Type ➪ Hyphenation (Figure 36).**

   The Hyphenation dialog box appears (**Figure 37**).

2. **Choose the On option.**

   This enables hyphenation throughout the entire document.

3. **Choose the way you want hyphenation to work:**

   Manual only: Hyphenated words occur only when you manually break them with Ctrl+Shift+hyphen.

   Manual plus dictionary: Words hyphenate with Ctrl+Shift+hyphen or if they are found in PageMaker's dictionary.

   Manual plus algorithm: Words hyphenate with Ctrl+Shift+hyphen or they break according to a built-in hyphenation algorithm.

4. **Click the OK button.**

   The hyphenation options are changed for the selected text (or all new text blocks, if no text was selected).

   As a rule, hyphenation should be used sparingly. You'll find that thin columns of text will require more hyphenation to avoid either excessive letter spacing or a large chunk of white space at the end of a line.

TIPS AND TRICKS

If you wish to change the hyphenation of existing text, select the text with the Text tool and change the hyphenation settings.

Hyphenation

83

To use spell checking:

1. **Click within the text block you wish to spell check using either the Text tool or Pointer tool (Figure 38).**

   If you select more than one text block (using the Pointer tool), you'll have to spell check each block separately.

2. **Choose Edit ⇨ Edit Story (Ctrl+E) (Figure 39).**

   The Story Editor window for that text block appears (**Figure 40**).

3. **Choose Utilities ⇨ Spelling (Ctrl+L) (Figure 41).**

   The Spelling dialog box appears (**Figure 42**).

4. **Click the Start button.**

   The spell checker will find the first word that has been spelled incorrectly (**Figure 43**).

   (continued on the following page)

Figure 38. Click the text block you wish to spell check.

Figure 39. Choose Edit Story from the Edit menu.

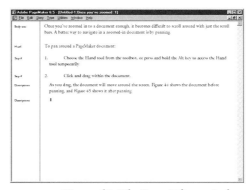

Figure 40. The Story Editor window.

Figure 41. Choose Spelling from the Utilities menu.

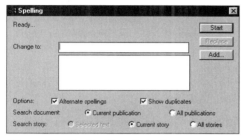

Figure 42. The Spelling dialog box.

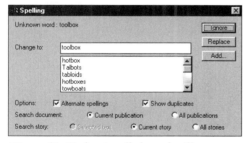

Figure 43. Each misspelled word will appear in turn.

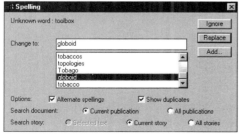

Figure 44. Choose the proper replacement word.

5. **Find the correctly spelled version of the word in the list box and click on that word (Figure 44).**

6. **Click the Replace button.**

   The word will be replaced with the correctly spelled version of the word and the next misspelled word will be highlighted.

7. **Replace each successive word with the correctly spelled version until the message "Spelling check complete" appears in the Spelling dialog box.**

8. **Close the Spelling dialog box.**

9. **Close the Story Editor window.**

Spell Checking

Word Counting

PageMaker allows you to count the number of words in a document. This is great if you're using PageMaker to create a geography report on South American capitals that must be at least 800 words. I'm sure there are other practical uses for it as well, I just can't think of any.

To count all the words in a document:

Choose Utilities ⇨ Plug-ins ⇨ Word Counter (**Figure 45**).

After some time, PageMaker will display a box providing all sorts of information about your document (**Figure 46**).

To count all the words in a text block:

1. Select the text block for which you wish to do a word count.

2. Choose Utilities ⇨ Plug-ins ⇨ Word Counter.

   PageMaker will display a box providing information about the selected text block.

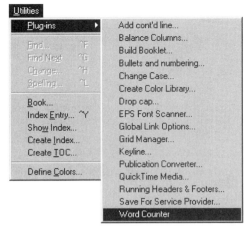

Figure 45. Choose Word Counter from the Plug-ins submenu.

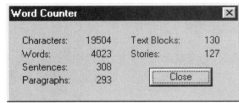

Figure 46. The Word Counter dialog box.

Figure 47. Choose Find from the Utilities menu.

Figure 48. The Find dialog box.

Figure 49. Each word will be highlighted when found.

To find a word in a text block:

1. Select the text block in which you want to find a word.

2. Choose Edit ⇨ Edit Story (Ctrl+E).

   The Story Editor window for that text block appears.

3. Choose Utilities ⇨ Find (Figure 47).

   The Find dialog box appears (Figure 48).

4. Enter the word you wish to find in the Find what text field.

5. Click the Find next button.

   That word (if it exists in that text block) will be highlighted in the Story Editor (Figure 49).

Finding Words

Find the next occurrence of the same word that has just been found by pressing Ctrl+G.

To replace one word with another:

1. Select the text block in which you wish to replace text.

2. Choose Edit ⇨ Edit Story (Ctrl+E).

   The Story Editor window for that text block appears.

3. Choose Utilities ⇨ Change (Figure 50).

   The Change dialog box appears (Figure 51). Change is just like Find, except you can choose to replace the word you find with another word.

4. Enter the word you wish to replace in the Find what text field.

5. Enter the word you wish to replace the found word with in the Change to text field.

6. Click the Find button.

   That word (if it can be found in that text block) will be highlighted in the Story Editor.

7. Click the Change button.

   The highlighted word will be replaced with the Change to word in the Story Editor (Figure 52).

Figure 50. Choose Change from the Utilities menu.

Figure 51. The Change dialog box.

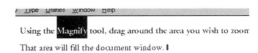

Figure 52. The changed word highlighted in the Story Editor.

Ah, the heart of a book really lies in its characters. Their deepest desires, their hidden passions. The complex web woven by the interactions of each character...

When we talk about characters in PageMaker, we're talking about letters, numbers, and anything else you can type with a single keystroke. Entering, editing, and formatting characters are a substantial part of working in PageMaker.

Characters vs. paragraphs

PageMaker treats characters quite differently than it does paragraphs, so it's a good idea to understand the differences and the similarities between the two.

Characters are:

- **One or more letters, numbers or symbols, including "invisible" characters such as spaces, tabs, and paragraph returns**

- **Formatted with fonts, character styles (bold, italic, etc.), point sizes, and vertical positions**

Paragraphs are:

- **The characters up to and including one paragraph return.**

- **Ended with a paragraph return.**

- **Formatted with alignments, indents, and space between paragraphs.**

What's the difference between a paragraph and a few hundred characters? Nothing, if there's no paragraph return. Once a paragraph return enters the mix (by pressing the Return key on your keyboard), the characters are split into two paragraphs (even if there's no text after or before the paragraph return).

Paragraph returns define paragraphs. Paragraph attributes affect *entire* paragraphs at one time. Triple-click on a text area and you'll select one entire Paragraph.

Invisible characters

Invisible characters are characters which you can't see, but which serve a function within a text block.

Common invisible characters are:

Paragraph returns

Spaces

Tabs

Line breaks

Column breaks

To display invisible characters:

1. **Choose Edit ⇨ Edit Story (Ctrl+E).**

   The Story Editor appears.

2. **Choose Story ⇨ Display ¶**

   All the special characters appear in the Story Editor window (**Figure 1**).

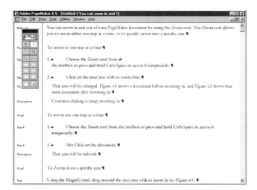

Figure 1. *The Story Editor is the only place you can view "invisible" characters.*

Original	Style
Bold	**Bold**
Italic	*Italic*
Bold Italic	***Bold Italic***
Underline	<u>Underline</u>
Reverse	Reverse
Strikethrough	~~Strikethrough~~
Small Caps	SMALL CAPS
Large Caps	LARGE CAPS
Superscript	Superscript
Subscript	Subscript

Figure 2. The style character attributes.

Figure 3. Choose Character from the Type menu.

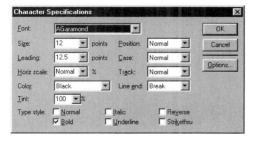

Figure 4. The Character Specifications dialog box.

Character attributes

Character attributes can be modified in either the Character Specifications dialog box, the Character Control palette, or by using a keyboard command. The following qualify as character attributes:

- **Font**

- **Point Size**

- **Leading**

- **Horizontal Scale**

- **Tracking**

- **Kerning**

- **Baseline Shift**

- **Character Attribute Styles**

- **Color/Tint**

The character attribute styles which can be modified in PageMaker are shown in **Figure 2**.

To modify character attributes:

1. **Select the characters you wish to modify.**

2. **Choose Type ➪ Character (Figure 3).**
   The Character Specifications dialog box appears (**Figure 4**).
   You can also press Ctrl+T (for "type") to access this dialog box.

Character Attributes

To modify character attributes using the Character Control palette:

1. Select the characters you wish to modify.

2. Choose Window⇨Show Control Palette (Figure 5) if the Control Palette isn't showing.

   The Character Control palette is shown in **Figure 6**.

   You can toggle between the Character Control palette and the Paragraph Control palette by clicking the "T" and "¶" buttons on the Control palette.

Figure 5. Choose Show Control Palette from the Window menu.

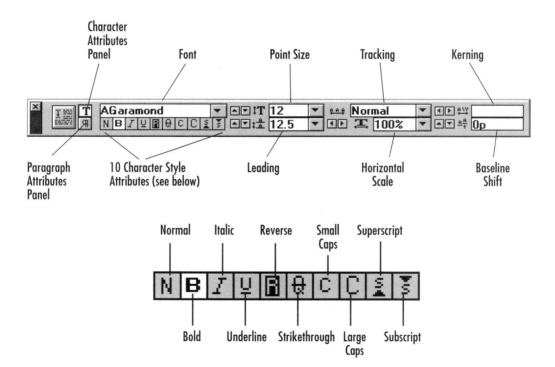

Figure 6. The entire Character Control palette (top), and its character attributes (bottom).

Figure 7. Select the characters you want to change.

Figure 8. Choose a font from the Character Control palette font pop-up menu.

Figure 9. The characters you selected will change to the chosen font.

To change the font:

1. **Select the characters you wish to change (Figure 7).**

   Only characters that are highlighted will be affected, as is the case with all character attribute modifications.

2. **Choose a font from the font listing on the Character Control palette (Figure 8).**

   When you release the mouse button, the font of the selected characters will change to match the font you've chosen (**Figure 9**).

 **TIPS AND TRICKS**

Sometimes it can be faster to choose a font (especially if you have many installed) by highlighting the font field and typing the first few letters of the font you want; PageMaker fills in the rest as you type.

 TIPS AND TRICKS

The techniques and examples you'll find throughout the rest of this book might be a little surprising. Instead of showing the common textbook examples and "proper" procedures for making changes or modifications, you'll learn the *best* way to make those changes. Many books would instruct you to change the font in the Character Specifications dialog box. Not here; in the real world the Character Specifications dialog box has only a few good uses, and changing fonts isn't one of them. The method shown here—using the Character Control palette—is the best way to change fonts. Since anything else is "worse," I won't even mention those "other" options. I think you'll appreciate the difference.

Changing Fonts

Bold and italic styles are unique among the many styles that can be applied to characters. While the other styles modify the character's font, bold and italic, when used properly, actually *change* the font.

For instance, when bold is applied to Adobe Garamond, Adobe Garamond Semibold is used in its place.

To make characters bold:

1. Select the characters you wish to bold (**Figure 10**).

2. Click the B button on the Character Control palette (**Figure 11**).

   The selected characters change to bold (**Figure 12**).

To make characters italic:

1. Select the characters you wish to italicize (**Figure 13**).

2. Click the I button on the Character Control palette (**Figure 14**).

   The selected characters change to italic (**Figure 15**).

Figure 10. Select the characters you wish to bold.

Figure 11. Click the B button on the Character Control palette or press Ctrl+Shift+B.

Figure 12. The selected characters become bold.

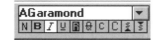

Figure 13. Select the characters you wish to italicize.

Figure 14. Click the I button on the Character Control palette or press Ctrl+Shift+I.

Figure 15. The selected characters are italicized.

🅿 TIPS AND TRICKS

Bold and italic are designed to work by looking for a "linked" font. If that font isn't found, the effect may appear correct on screen, but it will not print correctly. If you don't know which of your fonts have bold and italic faces, test them before using them for important work.

Normal

Italic Underlines

Reversed Strikethrough

Bold Underline

Italic Strikethrough

Underlined Reversed

Bold Italic

Figure 16. Various combinations of character styles.

Other font stylings are shown below, with short descriptions. In addition to each of the "basic" styles, you can combine styles to create such monstrosities as "bold outline superscript" and "italic shadow reverse." **Figure 16** shows several examples of these combinations.

Underline

Underlined text is great for headings, or as an alternative to italics. Ctrl+Shift+U.

Reverse

Reversed text is really (in the case of standard black text) just white type, which needs a dark background in order to be visible. Ctrl+Shift+V.

Strikethrough

Strikethrough text is relatively useless. Ctrl+Shift+/.

Small caps

Small caps is a font styling that changes lowercase letters into small versions of uppercase letters. Traditionally, these small letters had the same thickness as their larger counterparts, giving text an even feel. However, PageMaker's small caps feature cuts corners (as does all desktop publishing/graphics software) when it comes to small caps. Instead of substituting characters of the proper thickness, PageMaker uses reduced uppercase letters, making the thickness of strokes uneven (the uppercase letters are thick while the lowercase letters are thin).

To make characters into small caps:

1. Select the characters you wish to change to small caps (**Figure 17**).

2. Click the small caps icon (the lowercase c) on the Character Control palette (**Figure 18**).

   Lowercase letters of the selected characters are changed into small caps (**Figure 19**).

Figure 17. The text before small caps has been applied to it. Note that the widths of the strokes of the letters are the same.

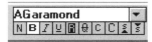

Figure 18. Click the Small Caps option in the Character Control palette.

TIPS AND TRICKS

You can change the reduction percentage of small caps by choosing Type⇨Character to display the Character Specifications dialog box. Click the Options button, and a text field will be available for changing the small caps percentage.

TALL ORDER

Figure 19. The text after small caps has been applied to it. Note that the widths of the strokes of the letters are different; the T and O are thicker than the other letters.

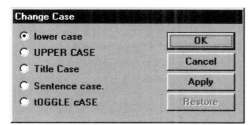

Figure 20. The Change Case dialog box.

Because Toulouse was the smartest cat, he knew he was better looking than Static or Sage.

because toulouse was the smartest cat, he knew he was better looking than static or sage.

BECAUSE TOULOUSE WAS THE SMARTEST CAT, HE KNEW HE WAS BETTER LOOKING THAN STATIC OR SAGE.

Because Toulouse Was The Smartest Cat, He Knew He Was Better Looking Than Static Or Sage.

Because toulouse was the smartest cat, he knew he was better looking than static or sage.

bECAUSE tOULOUSE WAS THE SMARTEST CAT, HE KNEW HE WAS BETTER LOOKING THAN sTATIC OR sAGE.

Figure 21. Original text (top) and each of the change case options, from top to bottom: lower case, UPPER CASE, Title Case, Sentence case, tOGGLE cASE.

There are two types of case changes in PageMaker: character attribute style case changes, which are turned on and off by clicking a button in the Character Control palette (as shown on the previous page for small caps), and Automatic "permanent" case changes, which are done through a plug-in called, appropriately, Change Case.

The major difference between the two methods is that character attribute changes keep the original case intact; you can always "turn off" small caps or large caps and your upper and lowercase characters will appear the way you typed them. Automatic case changing, on the other hand, *permanently* changes the characters; there is no "revert" back to what was originally typed/imported.

To automatically change case:

1. **Select the characters you wish to change.**

2. **Choose Utilities ⇨Plug-ins ⇨ Change Case.**

   The Change Case dialog box appears (**Figure 20**).

3. **Select the case option from the list of available options.**

   Figure 21 shows original text and what happens when each of the five case changes are applied to it.

4. **Click the OK button.**

   The selected text is changed to the case you specified.

Superscript and subscript

Superscript is a text format used to make characters smaller and to raise them up above the baseline. It is often used for footnotes and special symbols that appear within text, as shown in **Figure 22**.

Subscript is just like superscript, except that instead of moving the text up, it moves it down slightly, below the baseline. Subscript text is often used for chemical notations, as shown in **Figure 23**.

To make text superscript:

1. Select the characters you wish to change to superscript.

2. Click the superscript icon (the s with a small triangle below it) on the Character Control palette.

   All the selected characters will become superscript.

To make text subscript:

1. Select the characters you wish to change to subscript (**Figure 24**).

2. Click the subscript icon (the s with a small triangle above it) on the Character Control palette (**Figure 25**).

   All the selected characters will become subscript (**Figure 26**).

Bezier™ Inc.®

$$Bezier^{TM} \ Inc.^{®}$$

Figure 22. The ™ and ® are superscript, making them smaller and positioned above the baseline.

$$C0_2H_2Kr_3$$

Figure 23. The 2s and 3 are subscript, allowing me to create Kryptonite soda, which while refreshing, is sure to put Superman down for the count.

A great source of Acrobat 3 information is Ted Alspach's Acrobat 3 Visual QuickStart Guide buy it, published by Peachpit Press.

Figure 24. Select the characters you wish to make subscript.

Figure 25. Click the Subscript icon on the Character Control palette.

A great source of Acrobat 3 information is Ted Alspach's Acrobat 3 Visual QuickStart Guide buy it, published by Peachpit Press.

Figure 26. The selected characters are subscripted. In addition, I kerned the comma and subscripted letters drastically to give the words a subliminal feel (see page 102).

The Life and Times of

the Wonder Dog

Figure 27. Select the text you wish to make wider or thinner.

Figure 28. Click the T next to the Horizontal Scale field to highlight the Horizontal Scale.

The Life and Times of
Yoté
the Wonder Dog

Figure 29. The word "Yoté" has been horizontally scaled to 200% of its original width.

Horizontal scaling

PageMaker lets you make text wider and thinner by using the horizontal scaling control, found on the Character Control palette. You can make something as skinny as 5% of its original width:

or as wide as 250% of its original width:

Wide Load!

Of course, these extreme adjustments should only be made when there's a good reason, such as in small amounts for changing the width of type to make it fit better in a column, or to give headline type a special look.

To change the horizontal scale of text:

1. Select the characters you wish to make wider or thinner (**Figure 27**).

2. Click the T with a double-ended arrow under it on the Character Control palette (**Figure 28**).

   The value in the Horizontal Scale text field will be highlighted.

3. Type in a new value and press Enter.

   The text will be scaled horizontally to the size you specified (**Figure 29**).

Horizontally Scaling Text

Using Baseline Shift

Baseline shift

Baseline shift moves selected characters up and down on the baseline (the imaginary line that the bottom of most characters rests on), something akin to the way leading works (see the next page), but for one or more characters at a time.

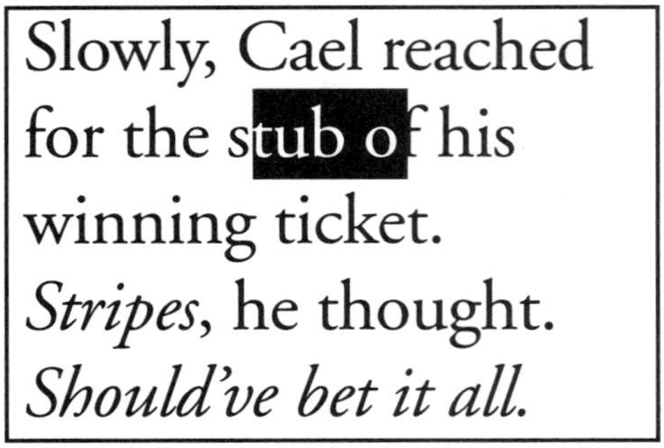

To change the baseline shift:

1. **Select the characters you wish to move up or down along the baseline (Figure 30).**

2. **Double-click the baseline shift text field, in the lower right of the Character Control palette.**

   The text field is highlighted (**Figure 31**). By default, the value for baseline shift is 0 (zero).

3. **Enter the distance you want the characters to move up or down.**

   Enter a positive number to move that distance *above* the baseline, and a negative number to move that distance *below* the baseline.

4. **Press the Enter key.**

   The selected characters will move up or down according to the amount you entered (**Figure 32**).

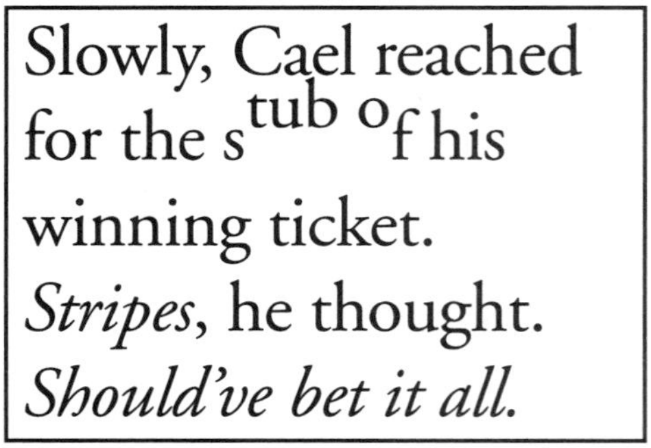

Slowly, Cael reached for the stub of his winning ticket. *Stripes*, he thought. *Should've bet it all.*

Figure 30. Highlight the text you wish to move up or down.

Figure 31. Double-click the baseline shift text field on the Character Control palette.

Slowly, Cael reached for the s^tub o_f his winning ticket. *Stripes*, he thought. *Should've bet it all.*

Figure 32. The selected characters will move by the amount entered in the baseline shift text field. In this case, the value was 0p9 (9 points).

> Slowly, Cael reached
> for the stub of his
> winning ticket.
> *Stripes,* he thought.
> *Should've bet it all.*

Figure 33. Highlight the text that needs a leading adjustment.

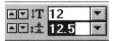

Figure 34. Double-click the leading text field on the Character Control palette.

> Slowly, Cael reached_
> |
>   60 pts.
> for the stub of his | _
>
> winning ticket.
> *Stripes,* he thought.
> *Should've bet it all.*

Figure 35. The line with the selected characters on it gains space both above and below the entire line. In this case the leading was changed to 60 pts. from 24 pts.

Leading

Leading is the distance between the baselines of consecutive lines of type. The greater the leading value, the more space appears between individual lines of text.

To adjust the leading:

1. **Select the characters in the line in which you wish to adjust the leading (Figure 33).**

2. **Double-click the leading text field in the Character Control palette.**

   The text field will become highlighted (**Figure 34**).

3. **Enter the amount of space you want above and below the line in which characters have been selected.**

   The leading value affects the line with the selected characters, moving it down (**Figure 35**). Lines below this line are moved down by the same amount as the leading value. The first line (which wasn't selected) seems to have additional space before it, but this space is actually the result of adding the depth of the leading amount (the portion that goes below the baseline) to the 24 point leading of the next line.

   If this seems confusing to you, you're not alone. PageMaker, by all rights, *shouldn't* let you adjust leading on a per line basis. Select entire paragraphs when making leading changes.

Kerning

Kerning is the process of changing the space between two characters. Some characters demand this treatment, such as a capital "T" in front of any lowercase letter without an ascender (acegmnopqrsuvwxyz).

To kern two letters together:

1. Click between the two letters you want to kern together (**Figure 36**).

2. Press Ctrl+Backspace to remove space between the letters.

   Continue pressing Ctrl+Backspace until the desired amount of space exists between the pair of characters (**Figure 37**). If you decide you've gone too far, you can increase the amount of space between the letters by pressing Ctrl+Shift+Backspace.

To kern two letters apart:

1. Click between the two letters you want to kern apart.

2. Press Ctrl+Shift+Backspace to add space between the letters.

   Continue pressing Ctrl+Shift+ Backspace until the correct amount of space exists between the characters. If you decide you've gone too far and added too much space, you can decrease the amount of space between the letters by pressing Ctrl+Backspace.

Figure 36. Click between the letters you wish to kern together.

Figure 37. After pressing Ctrl+Backspace three times, the space between the A and v is reduced significantly.

P TIPS AND TRICKS

The Ctrl+Shift+Backspace keystroke was used in this book to create an amount of space that "looked good" between menu names and the hollow arrow used between them. It's a subtle difference, but one that makes the book look better overall. Here's the untouched version:

File⇨Save

and after adding space before the arrow:

File ⇨Save

If a cat always lands on its feet, and **buttered toast always lands butter side down**, what would happen if you dropped a cat with buttered toast strapped to its back?

Figure 38. Select the characters to which you wish to apply tracking.

Figure 39. Choose a tracking setting from the tracking pop-up menu on the Character Control palette.

If a cat always lands on its feet, and **buttered toast always lands butter side down,** what would happen if you dropped a cat with buttered toast strapped to its back?

Figure 40. After entering a tracking value of Tight to the selected text, the text is tightened.

Tracking

Tracking is the process of removing (or sometimes adding) space between *all* the characters in a word, a line, a paragraph, or even an entire story.

To change the tracking:

1. Select the characters whose tracking you wish to change (**Figure 38**).

2. Choose a different tracking setting from the tracking pop-up menu on the Character Control palette (**Figure 39**).

   The tracking of the selected characters will change (**Figure 40**).

   There are six different settings for tracking, shown in **Figure 41**.

   For most of the text in this book, tracking was set to Normal.

Spacing Out Letters with Tracking

No Track
Very Loose
Loose
Normal
Tight
Very Tight

Figure 41. The six different tracking settings.

To color characters:

1. Select the characters you'd like to color (Figure 42).

2. Display the Colors palette by choosing Window⇨Show Colors (Ctrl+J) (Figure 43).

   The Colors palette appears (**Figure 44**).

3. Click on the color you want to change the selected characters to.

   The characters change to the color you selected in the palette (**Figure 45**).

   Colors are discussed in detail in Chapter 14.

Figure 42. Select the characters whose color you wish to change.

Figure 43. *Choose Show Colors from the Window menu.*

Figure 44. *The Colors palette.*

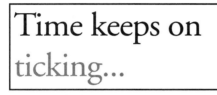

Figure 45. *The characters are now the color you picked (even though it's hard to see on a black and white page like this one).*

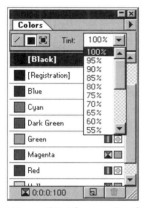

Figure 46. Select the characters you wish to tint.

Figure 47. Choose a tint from the pop-up menu in the Colors palette.

SageMonster

Figure 48. The characters (all were selected in this example) are changed to 65% of their original color.

55%	0%	55%	0%	55%
	60%	5%	60%	5%	60%
10%	65%	10%	65%	10%	65%
15%	70%	15%	70%	15%	70%
20%	75%	20%	75%	20%	75%
25%	80%	25%	80%	25%	80%
30%	85%	30%	85%	30%	85%
35%	90%	35%	90%	35%	90%
40%	95%	40%	95%	40%	
45%	100%		100%	45%	
50%				50%	

Figure 49. Tints of black on different backgrounds.

Tinting characters

You can tint any text color from 0% (white) to 100% (the actual color). This is a great way to give the illusion that a printed piece has more colors than it actually does.

To tint characters:

1. Select the characters you want to tint (**Figure 46**).

2. Display the Colors palette by choosing Window⇨Show Colors (**Ctrl+J**).

   The Colors palette appears. Pressing Ctrl+J while the Colors palette is displayed will hide this palette.

3. Choose a tint from the Tint pop-up menu at the top of the palette (**Figure 47**).

   The characters change to the tint you selected in the menu (**Figure 48**).

   Figure 49 shows how the different tints of black appear on a white background, a gray background, and a black background.

Tinting Characters

105

Special characters

To use special characters (those that don't appear on your keyboard), you need to enter a special code that PageMaker will turn into the desired character. **Figure 50** (on the following page) shows all of these codes.

To enter a special character:

1. Place the blinking insertion point cursor where you would like the special character to be.

2. Press the Alt key.
   Keep the Alt key pressed down until you've finished step 3.

3. Enter the four digit code from the chart on the next page.

4. Release the Alt key.
   The special character will appear in your text block.

ƒ	0131	-	0173	×	0215
„	0132	®	0174	Ø	0216
…	0133	¯	0175	Ù	0217
†	0134	°	0176	Ú	0218
‡	0135	±	0177	Û	0219
ˆ	0136	²	0178	Ü	0220
‰	0137	³	0179	Ý	0221
Š	0138	´	0180	ß	0222
‹	0139	µ	0181	à	0223
Œ	0140	¶	0182	à	0224
	0141	·	0183	á	0225
	0142	¸	0184	â	0226
	0143	¹	0185	ã	0227
	0144	º	0186	ä	0228
'	0145	»	0187	å	0229
'	0146	¼	0188	æ	0230
"	0147	½	0189	ç	0231
"	0148	¾	0190	è	0232
•	0149	¿	0191	é	0233
–	0150	À	0192	ê	0234
—	0151	Á	0193	ë	0235
˜	0152	Â	0194	ì	0236
™	0153	Ã	0195	í	0237
š	0154	Ä	0196	î	0238
›	0155	Å	0197	ï	0239
œ	0156	Æ	0198	ð	0240
	0157	Ç	0199	ñ	0241
	0158	È	0200	ò	0242
Ÿ	0159	É	0201	ó	0243
	0160	Ê	0202	ô	0244
¡	0161	Ë	0203	õ	0245
¢	0162	Ì	0204	ö	0246
£	0163	Í	0205	÷	0247
¤	0164	Î	0206	ø	0248
¥	0165	Ï	0207	ù	0249
¦	0166	Ð	0208	ú	0250
§	0167	Ñ	0209	û	0251
¨	0168	Ò	0210	ü	0252
©	0169	Ó	0211	ý	0253
ª	0170	Ô	0212	þ	0254
«	0171	Õ	0213	ÿ	0255
¬	0172	Ö	0214		

Figure 50. Special characters and the codes that should be entered while pressing Alt to access them.

PARAGRAPHS AND TABS

Paragraph and tab formatting are somewhat unusual processes in PageMaker. When any character within a paragraph is selected (or even if an insertion point is within that paragraph), the entire paragraph is affected by paragraph and tab formatting.

Introduction to Paragraphs and Tabs

Paragraph attributes

Paragraph attributes, which affect entire paragraphs at a time, are the following:

Horizontal Alignment: Flush Left, Flush Right, Centered, Justified, and Force Justified.

Indents: Left Indent, Right Indent, First Line Indent.

Paragraph Space: Space before, Space after.

Paragraph Rules: Rules above, Rules below.

Paragraph Options: Keep lines together, Column break before, Page break before, Table of Contents inclusion.

Tabs: Left, Right, Center, Decimal

Tab Leaders: Characters that appear in the tab space, such as ... and __.

Styles: Contain paragraph and character attributes, but applied to entire paragraphs at one time.

Paragraph formatting

Paragraphs are formatted with paragraph attributes either by placing the blinking insertion point anywhere within the paragraph, or by selecting any number of characters (including the paragraph return character) within a paragraph. Then choose the Paragraph Specifications dialog box, an option in the Paragraph Control palette, or press a paragraph attribute keyboard command.

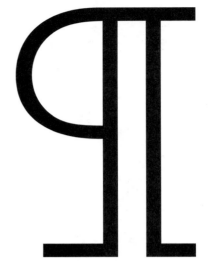

***Figure 1.** The paragraph break symbol in epic proportions.*

Paragraph definition

Paragraphs are defined by paragraph breaks, not to be confused with line breaks. Paragraph breaks are actual characters typed by pressing the Return key (Enter on some keyboards).

If a text block contains no paragraph breaks, it is one paragraph. If it contains one paragraph break, it is two paragraphs. In fact, the number of paragraphs is always one more than the number of paragraph breaks. Even if there isn't any text per se in a paragraph, it is still considered a paragraph by PageMaker.

Paragraph returns appear as ¶ in the Story Editor (but not in the main PageMaker window).

The Paragraph Specifications dialog box

The Paragraph Specifications dialog box (**Figure 2**) is the nerve center for most paragraph-specific controls and formatting. While paragraph controls can also be found in the Type menu and the Paragraph Control palette, the Paragraph Specifications dialog box contains *everything* for general paragraph formatting.

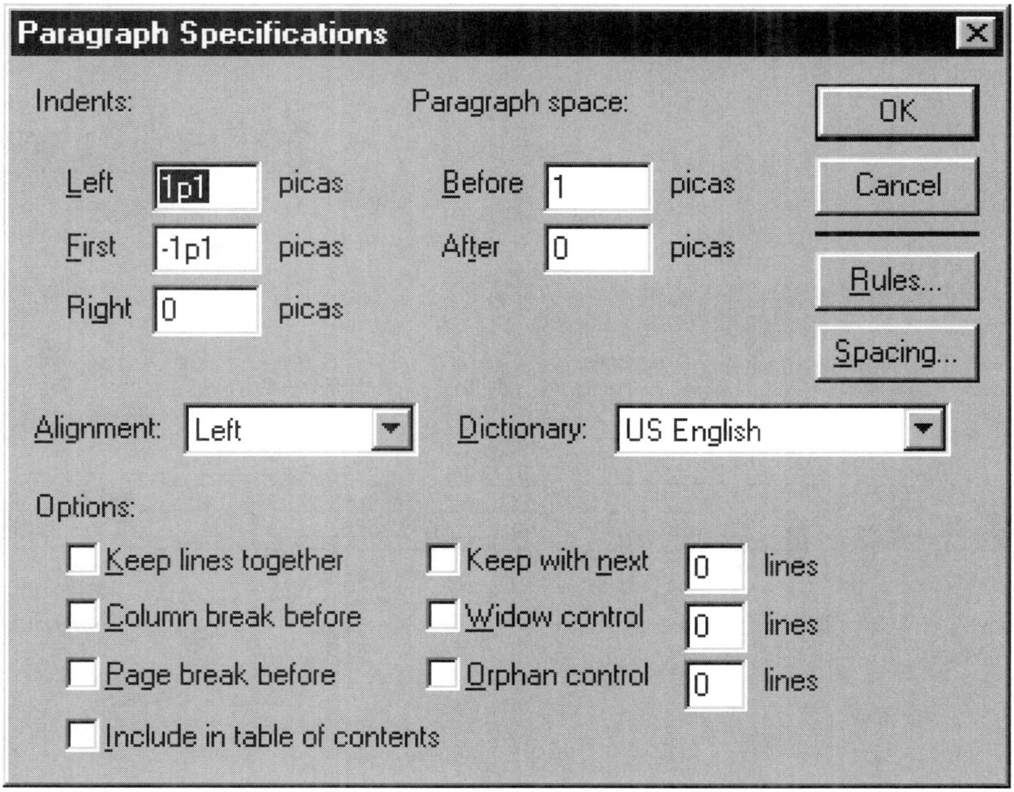

Figure 2. The Paragraph Specifications dialog box.

The Paragraph Control palette

The Paragraph Control palette includes many of the most commonly used paragraph controls.

To display the Paragraph Control palette:

1. Choose Window⇨Show Control Palette (Ctrl+') (**Figure 3**).

   The Control palette will appear.

2. If the Control palette doesn't look like the one in Figure 5, click the Paragraph Attributes button (**¶**) (**Figure 4**).

   The Paragraph attributes will appear on the Control palette (**Figure 5**).

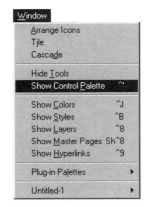

Figure 3. *Choose Show Control Palette from the Window menu.*

Figure 4. *Click the Paragraph Attributes button.*

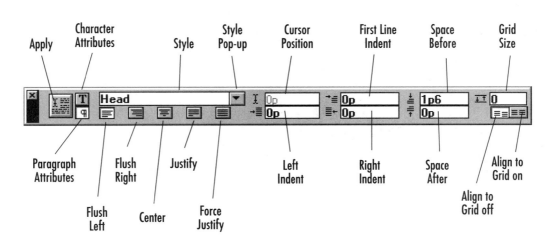

Figure 5. *The Paragraph features of the Control palette.*

Flush left

You would expect an area commonly referred to as Bloody Basin to be devoid of human life. However, the towns of Mordor (how fitting), Dead Crow Pass, and Clay Crossing all lay within its bounds.

Flush right

You would expect an area commonly referred to as Bloody Basin to be devoid of human life. However, the towns of Mordor (how fitting), Dead Crow Pass, and Clay Crossing all lay within its bounds.

Center

You would expect an area commonly referred to as Bloody Basin to be devoid of human life. However, the towns of Mordor (how fitting), Dead Crow Pass, and Clay Crossing all lay within its bounds.

Justify

You would expect an area commonly referred to as Bloody Basin to be devoid of human life. However, the towns of Mordor (how fitting), Dead Crow Pass, and Clay Crossing all lay within its bounds.

Force justify

You would expect an area commonly referred to as Bloody Basin to be devoid of human life. However, the towns of Mordor (how fitting), Dead Crow Pass, and Clay Crossing all lay within its bounds.

Figure 6. The five Alignment options.

Horizontal Alignment

Text can be set so that the text block is flush left (like most of the text in this book), flush right, centered, justified, or force justified.

To change the alignment of a paragraph:

1. **Place your cursor anywhere within the paragraph you want to change.**

   You can also select a character, or select the entire paragraph by triple-clicking on the paragraph.

2. **Choose an alignment from the buttons on the Paragraph Control palette.**

   The entire paragraph alignment is changed to the one you've selected.

Figure 6 shows the same paragraph set to each of the Alignment options.

P TIPS AND TRICKS

Much quicker, and fairly easy to learn, are the keyboard commands for changing alignment:

Flush left: Ctrl+Shift+L

Flush right: Ctrl+Shift+R

Center: Ctrl+Shift+C

Justify: Ctrl+Shift+J

Force justify: Ctrl+Shift+F

Changing Horizontal Alignment

113

Indents

Each paragraph in PageMaker can be indented in three ways:

Left indent: This is how far from the left edge of the text block the left side of the text is located.

Right indent: This is how far from the right edge of the text block the right side of the text is located.

First line indent: This special indent controls how far the first line of a paragraph is indented from the left indent.

All of these values are 0 (zero) by default.

To change the indents of a paragraph:

1. Place your cursor anywhere within the paragraph (Figure 7).

2. Double-click on the left indent text field (Figure 8) and enter the value from the left side of the text block you want to indent the text.

3. Press the Tab key to highlight the next field, and change the First Line Indent value of the paragraph.

4. Press the Tab key again to highlight the right indent value (Figure 9), and enter a new value.

5. Press the Enter key to finalize your changes.

   The new indents appear in the paragraph(s) you have chosen (**Figure 10**).

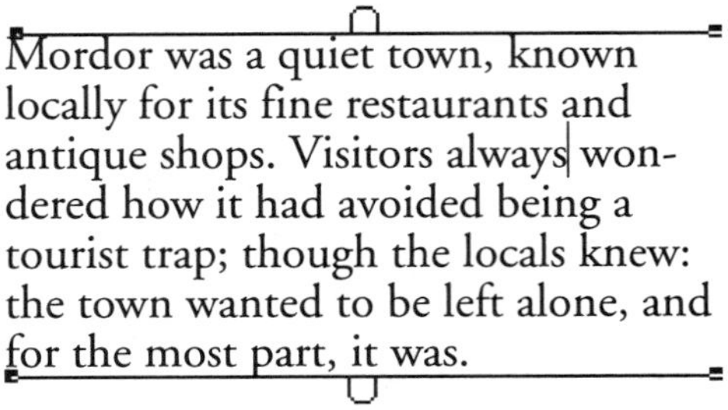

Mordor was a quiet town, known locally for its fine restaurants and antique shops. Visitors always wondered how it had avoided being a tourist trap; though the locals knew: the town wanted to be left alone, and for the most part, it was.

Figure 7. Place your cursor anywhere within the paragraph you wish to change.

Figure 8. Double-click on the left indent text field in the Control palette and enter a new value.

Figure 9. Tab over to the right indent text field.

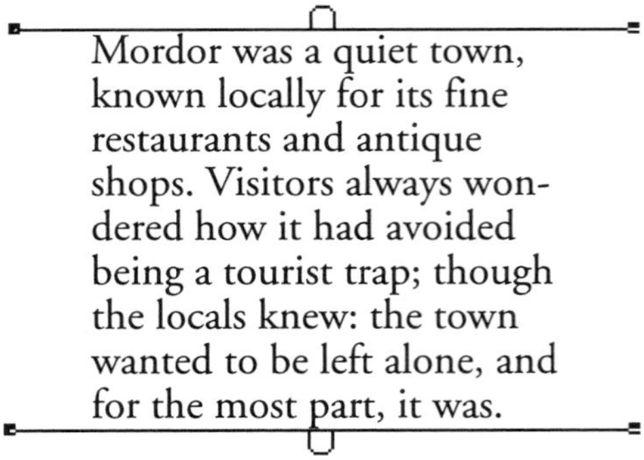

Mordor was a quiet town, known locally for its fine restaurants and antique shops. Visitors always wondered how it had avoided being a tourist trap; though the locals knew: the town wanted to be left alone, and for the most part, it was.

Figure 10. A text block, after applying a left indent of 2p and a right indent of 1p.

Indents

Possibly the most remarkable characteristic of Clay Crossing was the abundance of giant red rock cliffs, the southernmost collection (and possibly one of the most beautiful) in Arizona.

Figure 11. This text has a left indent of 2p, and a first line indent of -2p.

TIPS AND TRICKS

Hanging indents are often used for bulleted or numbered lists. To create such a list, place a bullet (or number, or whatever) before the paragraph, and then type a tab. In the Indents dialog box (see later in this chapter), set a standard left tab where the left indent marker is. When you set the hanging indent, the bullet will be "floating" off to the left of the paragraph, as shown below.

- Bullets are often used for hanging indents.
- You would think rope would be used instead.

Hanging indents

A *hanging indent* is when the first line of a paragraph sticks out to the left of the rest of the paragraph (**Figure 11**).

The key to hanging indents is that they must have a first line indent with a negative value, which can't exceed the (positive) value of the left indent.

For instance, a paragraph with a left indent of 1p could have a hanging indent of -1p (hanging indents are set in the first line indent text field). In this case, the first line of the paragraph would be even with the left edge of the text block, but the rest of the paragraph would align 1p right from the left edge.

To create a hanging indent:

1. Place your cursor within the paragraph you want to change.

2. Enter a value in the left indent text field in the Paragraph Control palette.

   In order to have a hanging indent, you *must* have a left indent greater than 0 (zero).

3. Press Tab, and enter a negative number in the first line indent text field.

   You can enter a value up to the number entered as the left indent, but no greater. Entering the inverse of the left indent (if the left indent is 3p6, you would enter -3p6) will result in the first line being even with the left edge of the text block.

Hanging Indents

Spacing between paragraphs

You can add space between paragraphs by using additional paragraph returns, or by using the Paragraph Spacing controls to add space before or after a paragraph.

Let's get one thing straight right away: using additional paragraph returns *is* a bad thing. It may seem easier (heck, you're just whacking the Enter key, after all), but if you *ever* have to go back to that document to edit it, you'll be sorry. There are two problems with using paragraph returns to add space between paragraphs:

- **The height is predetermined, and changing it can only be done by adjusting leading.**

- **When text wraps to another column or page, the paragraph return may "push" it down further than it needs to be.**

On the other hand, using paragraph spacing can be done with just a click in the Paragraph Control palette and by entering how far down you want your paragraph to be (and how much space you want below it).

To add space between paragraphs:

1. Click within the paragraph you wish to change (Figure 12).

2. Click in the space before or space after text fields (Figure 13), and enter the amount of space in each, then press Enter.

Changes are shown in **Figure 14**.

The story of Burgundy is an old one, passed down from the first generation of Arizonan settlers to the current inhabitants of Bloody Basin:
A small|pack of settlers, heading west, stopped for the night in what is now known as Burgundy. When they awoke at the crack of dawn, they discovered that several of their horses had wandered off. A search party was formed, and the explorers set off looking for their missing horses. That evening, no horses had been recovered, and two of the explorers, brothers by the names of Jonathon and Martin Sands, had disappeared as well. The explorers chose to stay on until they could find the missing men.
Of course, they never *did* find them, but by the time they had given up, they had developed an odd fondness for Burgundy, and settled here. Soon one of them discovered copper just southeast of the town, and buildings went up like wildfire.

Figure 12. Place your cursor in the paragraph you wish to change.

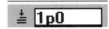

Figure 13. The space before text field in the Paragraph Control palette.

The story of Burgundy is an old one, passed down from the first generation of Arizonan settlers to the current inhabitants of Bloody Basin:

A small pack of settlers, heading west, stopped for the night in what is now known as Burgundy. When they awoke at the crack of dawn, they discovered that several of their horses had wandered off. A search party was formed, and the explorers set off looking for their missing horses.

That evening, no horses had been recovered, and two of the explorers, brothers by the names of Jonathon and Martin Sands, had disappeared as well. The explorers chose to stay on until they could find the missing men.
Of course, they never *did* find them, but by the time they had given up, they had developed an odd fondness for Burgundy, and settled here. Soon one of them discovered copper just southeast of the town, and buildings went up like wildfire.

Figure 14. The second paragraph, after applying a space before of 1p0 and a space after of 0p6.

Bloody Basin looked as Cael might have expected; the desert floor was reddish, almost brown, as it led up to the mountain ranges that bordered its sides. It reminded Cael of pictures he'd seen of the Painted Desert, but instead of being full of color and brightness, Bloody Basin was somber and dark, even under the cloudless sky this early in the morning.

Figure 15. Click within the paragraph above which you want a rule to appear.

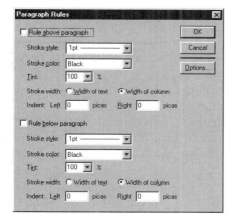

Figure 16. The Paragraph Rules dialog box.

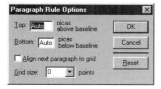

Figure 17. The Paragraph Rule Options dialog box.

Bloody Basin looked as Cael might have expected; the desert floor was reddish, almost brown, as it led up to the mountain ranges that bordered its sides. It reminded Cael of pictures he'd seen of the Painted Desert, but instead of being full of color and brightness, Bloody Basin was somber and dark, even under the cloudless sky this early in the morning.

Figure 18. The rule above the paragraph.

Paragraph rules

PageMaker allows you to place rules above and below each paragraph. This works nicely with PageMaker's space before and space after capabilities.

To create a rule above a paragraph:

1. **Place your cursor anywhere within the paragraph you wish to add a rule above (Figure 15).**

2. **Choose Type ⇨ Paragraph (Ctrl+M).**

   The Paragraph Specifications dialog box appears (**Figure 2**).

3. **Click the Rules button.**

   The Paragraph Rules dialog box appears (**Figure 16**).

4. **Check the Rule above paragraph box, and change any settings to the rule you would like to create.**

5. **Click the Options button.**

   The Paragraph Rule Options dialog box appears (**Figure 17**). Here you can set the offset distance of the rule from the top of the paragraph. I've chosen 2p (two picas) for this example. *Offset* refers to the amount of space between the text and the rule.

6. **Enter an offset value and click OK three times.**

   Each of the three dialog boxes will close, and there will now be a rule above the paragraph.(**Figure 18**).

Paragraph Rules

Paragraph spacing

PageMaker gives you complete control over how space is added (or removed) when paragraphs are justified. These controls are located in the Paragraph Spacing Attributes dialog box (**Figure 19**).

There are two primary types of spacing (**Figure 20**):

Word space: Word spacing controls the width of the space bar character. In essence, this determines the amount of space between words.

Letter space: This controls the space around each letter. The typographer who designed the font you're using has optimized the width of each letter and built in *kerning pairs* for specific sets of letters so that they always look nice together. But when text is justified, the increased (or decreased) word space can look odd. By allowing PageMaker to adjust letter space, justified text can be made to look more appealing.

To change the paragraph spacing:

1. **Click within the paragraph you wish to change.**

2. **Choose Type ⇨ Paragraph.**
   The Paragraph Specifications dialog box appears (**Figure 2**).

3. **Click the Spacing button.**
   The Paragraph Spacing Attributes dialog box appears.

4. **Enter any spacing changes into the dialog box and press OK twice.**

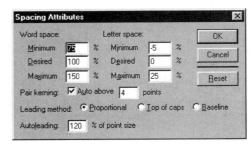

Figure 19. The Paragraph Spacing Attributes dialog box.

The ghost town of Pike's End was entirely empty. It was eerie that a complete town, with dozens of buildings and a few paved roads, could be this silent. Cael almost expected to see a chain link fence surrouding the outskirts of the town, but there was none.

The ghost town of Pike's End was entirely empty. It was eerie that a complete town, with dozens of buildings and a few paved roads, could be this silent. Cael almost expected to see a chain link fence surrouding the outskirts of the town, but there was none.

The ghost town of Pike's End was entirely empty. It was eerie that a complete town, with dozens of buildings and a few paved roads, could be this silent. Cael almost expected to see a chain link fence surrouding the outskirts of the town, but there was none.

Figure 20. The same three paragraphs with different spacing. The top paragraph has default spacing. The middle paragraph has only letter spacing, and the bottom paragraph has only word spacing.

The Saguaro Mine had collapsed in 1890, killing thirty people. Attempts at rescue caused another major collapse, killing nine of the rescue workers.

A team of explorers was said to have been lost in the 50's; they had told friends that they were going to try to find out what happened to all those people. Cael wasn't sure what to believe.

Figure 21. A widow appears at the bottom of the left column.

The Saguaro Mine had collapsed in 1890, killing thirty people. Attempts at rescue caused another major collapse, killing nine of the rescue workers, many of who had relatives that had been inside the mine at the time of its

collapse.

A team of explorers was said to have been lost in the 50's; they had told friends that they were going to try to find out what happened to all those people. Cael wasn't sure what to believe.

Figure 22. An orphan appears at the top of the right column.

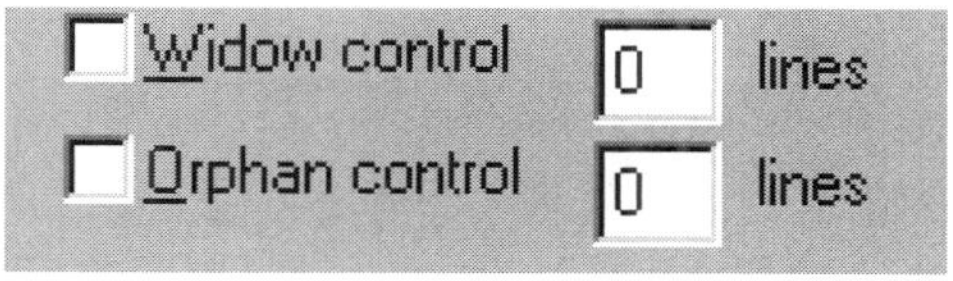

Figure 23. The Widow and Orphan control portion of the Paragraph Specifications dialog box.

Widows and orphans

No one likes widows and orphans— at least, not in PageMaker. A widow is the first line of a paragraph that falls at the bottom of a column (**Figure 21**). An orphan is the last line of a paragraph that falls at the top of a column (**Figure 22**).

PageMaker has built-in controls that allow you to specify how many lines of text from a paragraph can fall at the bottom or top of a column. If it finds one of the two despicable creatures, it moves a line (or more, depending on your settings) from the first column into the second one.

To change widow and orphan options:

1. **Click in the paragraph you wish to protect from widows and orphans.**

   In some cases, you might want to select all the text in a story to prevent widows and orphans throughout.

2. **Choose Type ⇨ Paragraph.**

   The Paragraph Specifications dialog box appears.

3. **Check the Widow control and Orphan control checkboxes and enter the smallest number of lines that you'll allow at the bottom (widows) and top (orphans) of any column of text.**

   I keep mine set at 3 for most of the work I do, so I never have less than three lines of a paragraph at the top or bottom of a column.

Changing Widow and Orphan Options

Tabs

Tabs are used to horizontally space type within a column. You can also use tabs to create "columns" of text within a text block.

By default, tabs occur at every half inch from the left edge of the text block. Here's an example:

Tab　　Tab　　Tab　　Tab

These default tabs are flush left, meaning that type aligns to the left edge of the tab stop. When you create a new tab stop, all the default tab stops to the left of the "custom" stop are erased. If I inserted a custom tab stop at about 1 1/4", it would look like:

TabTab　　Tab

Note that the default tab immediately following the custom tab (at the 1 1/2" mark) is still in place, as is the one at the 2" mark. If this column were wider, tabs would continue every half inch until the right edge of the text block.

Setting tabs

Tabs are set within the Indents/Tabs dialog box (**Figure 24**), which resembles and mostly acts like a floating palette, yet works like a dialog box (you have to click the OK button to do anything other than set tabs).

To set a new custom tab stop:

1. **Place your cursor within the paragraph you wish to place the tab.**

   Tabs are a form of paragraph attributes, and they affect the entire paragraph.

2. **Choose Type⇨Indents/Tabs (Ctrl+I).**

   The Indents/Tabs dialog box appears.

3. **Set your tabs and click OK.**

   The new tab settings take effect immediately after the box is closed.

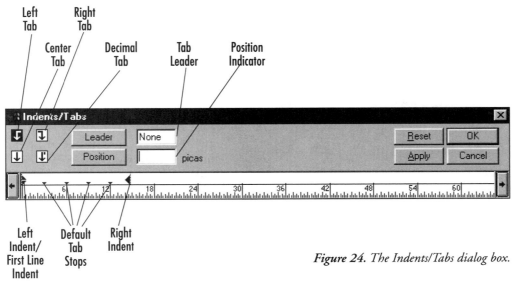

Figure 24. The Indents/Tabs dialog box.

City	Pop.	Elevation
Bell Town	320	1200.32
Bézier	11,500	600.2
Burgundy	390	1632.6
Swordshire	509	3021.04
Centura	82	380.62

Figure 25. This chart was created using only left tabs.

City	Pop.	Elevation
Bell Town	320	1200.32
Bézier	11,500	600.2
Burgundy	390	1632.6
Swordshire	509	3021.04
Centura	82	380.62

Figure 26. The same chart with right tabs.

City	Pop.	Elevation
Bell Town	320	1200.32
Bézier	11,500	600.2
Burgundy	390	1632.6
Swordshire	509	3021.04
Centura	82	380.62

Figure 27. The same chart with center tabs.

City	Pop.	Elevation
Bell Town	320	1200.32
Bézier	11,500	600.2
Burgundy	390	1632.6
Swordshire	509	3021.04
Centura	82	380.62

Figure 28. The same chart with decimal tabs.

Tab Types

There are four different tab types in PageMaker: left, right, center, and decimal.

Left tabs align text flush left to the tab, so that the text expands out to the right (**Figure 25**).

Right tabs align text flush right to the tab, so that text at that tab expands out to the left (**Figure 26**).

Center tabs align text to the center of the tab stop (**Figure 27**).

Decimal tabs align text to the first decimal within the text, or if there is no decimal, they act as right tabs (**Figure 28**).

You can, of course, mix tab types. **Figure 29** shows the same text with all four tab types.

City	Pop.	Elevation
Bell Town	320	1200.32
Bézier	11,500	600.2
Burgundy	390	1632.6
Swordshire	509	3021.04
Centura	82	380.62

Figure 29. All four tab types were used for this chart. Center tabs were used for the headings. Left tabs were used for the cities, right tabs for the population figures, and decimal tabs for the elevation.

Tab Types

121

Tab Leaders

Tab leaders (pronounced leeders, unlike leading, which is pronounced ledding) are strings of characters that fill the space before tabs. Any tab type can have a tab leader, and any character can be a tab leader.

Typically, you'll find tab leaders in a table of contents (**Figure 30**), on menus (**Figure 31**), or in any other list where some of the items might be horizontally far away from the other items on the same line. For the most part, tab leaders are periods, although you can use any character (**Figure 32**) as a tab leader.

To create a tab leader:

1. Click (or select) within the paragraph(s) you wish to contain the tab leader.

2. Choose Type⇨Indents/Tabs. The Indents/Tabs dialog box appears above the current column.

3. Select the tab (or create one if no custom tabs exist) that you want to be a tab leader.

4. Choose a setting from the tab leader pop-up menu or type in your own character as a tab leader.

5. Click the OK button.

Figure 30. One of the chapters from the original draft of this book, cut by my fearless editor.

The Verde Diner

Fish $3.00

Fish and Chips $4.50

Chips $2.00

Potatoes (Make your own chips) $1.00

Tater Tots .... $.20/ea

Tots (ages 2-4) .... $market

Figure 31. A menu with tab leaders.

Fish @@@@@@@@@@@@@@@@@ $3.00

Fish _____ $3.00

Fish ikikikikikikikikikikikikikikik $3.00

Fish ●●●●●●●●●●●●●●●●●●●●●● $3.00

Fish - $3.00

Figure 32. Different tab leaders were used for each line.

TIPS AND TRICKS

You can format tab leaders with any character attributes by selecting the leaders and then changing the font, size, etc. in the Character Control palette.

Using Tab Leaders

Many introductory PageMaker books treat styles as an after-thought or as an option best left to the experts. I think that's both condescending and wrong. Styles are easy to use and can save even the greenest user boatloads of time when working with a PageMaker document, and tenfold *that* when making document-wide changes and corrections.

Styles are paragraph-based, but they also involve character-based attributes. Because of their flexibility and time-saving benefits, I've given styles a chapter all their own.

Styles

Think of styles as containers holding most character and paragraph attributes. These containers can be applied to any paragraph with a single click.

And that's the true power of styles: being able to format a paragraph (or several paragraphs) with many different character and paragraph formats at once.

Think of how you typically apply formatting to paragraphs: first, the paragraph is selected. Then, each of the attributes is selected and modified in turn, until all the changes are complete. With a few changes, such as font, size, leading, tracking, and alignment, that can take up to a minute or more. Maybe that doesn't sound like much time—until you consider that formatting is almost a continuous procedure in PageMaker.

Styles can also automate your work in PageMaker, taking you from style to style automatically (via the handy Next Style function).

Styles can be created, edited, deleted, and applied within the Styles palette (**Figure 1**), accessed from the Window menu, or by pressing Ctrl+B.

Figure 1. The Styles palette, showing the styles used to create this book.

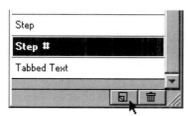

Figure 2. Click the New Style button to create a new style.

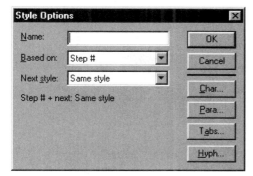

Figure 3. The Style Options dialog box, where you can name your new style.

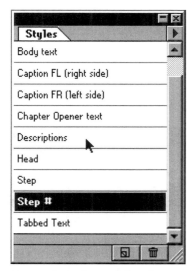

Figure 4. Apply a style by selecting text, then clicking on the style name in the Styles palette.

The following steps require that you have the Styles palette visible. You can display the Styles palette by pressing Ctrl+B, or by choosing Window➪Show Style.

To define a new style:

1. **Highlight the text you wish to use as a style.**

2. **Click the New Style button on the Styles palette (Figure 2).**
   This will display the Style Options dialog box (**Figure 3**).

3. **Enter a name for the new style.**
   Be as descriptive as you can.

4. **Click the OK button.**
   The new style will be added to the Styles palette and can be applied as shown below.

To apply a style:

1. **Place your cursor in the paragraph to which you wish to apply the style.**
   You can select text in several paragraphs to change all those paragraphs at once.

2. **Click the name of the style in the Styles palette (Figure 4).**
   The selected paragraphs will change to that style.

Defining and Applying Styles

The super-fast amazing style creation

You can use the Control palette to create styles quickly, even if you don't have the Styles palette showing. The paragraph display of the Control palette lists the current style—by typing over that style, you can name a new style almost instantly. Here's how it works:

To quickly create a new style:

1. Select some text that is representative of the style you wish to create.

2. Display the paragraph portion of the Control palette (**Figure 5**).

3. Highlight the style name in the Control palette (**Figure 6**).

   You can do this by double-clicking the style name or clicking to the left of the text field.

4. Type in a new name for the style you wish to create, and press Enter.

   A dialog box appears, asking if you're sure you want to create a new style (**Figure 7**).

5. Click the OK button.

   The new style is created.

Figure 5. Display the Paragraph Control palette.

Figure 6. Highlight the name of the current style.

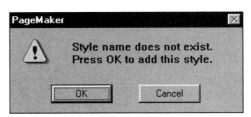

Figure 7. The dialog box that appears after you press Enter to create a new style.

You can apply any style without opening the Styles palette. Simply click and hold on the triangle to the right of the style name in the Paragraph Control palette, and select a style from the list that appears.

Figure 8. Double-click on the style you wish to modify.

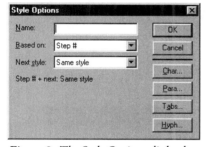

Figure 9. The Style Options dialog box.

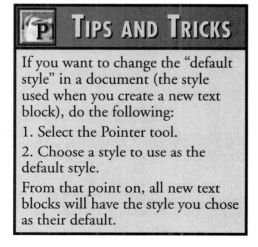

TIPS AND TRICKS

If you want to change the "default style" in a document (the style used when you create a new text block), do the following:

1. Select the Pointer tool.

2. Choose a style to use as the default style.

From that point on, all new text blocks will have the style you chose as their default.

To modify an existing style:

1. **Double-click on the style (in the Styles palette) that you wish to modify (Figure 8).**

   The Style Options dialog box appears (**Figure 9**).

2. **Click one of the buttons along the right side of the Style Options dialog box.**

   The corresponding dialog box will appear. For instance, clicking the Char button opens the Character Attributes dialog box, with settings for that style.

3. **Make your changes and click OK.**

   This returns you to the Style Options dialog box.

4. **Click the OK button.**

   Any uses of that style will be updated throughout the document.

   This is truly one of the most powerful capabilities of styles: when you make a change to the style, all the text "tagged" with that style is changed as well.

To duplicate an existing style:

1. **Drag the style (in the Styles palette) down to the New Style icon (Figure 10).**

   When you release the mouse button, the Style Options dialog box appears with the style name and the word "copy" after it in the Name text field (**Figure 11**).

2. **Rename the new style.**

   You *can* choose to keep the "style copy" name, but I wouldn't recommend it.

3. **Click the OK button.**

   The new style will be added to the Styles palette.

To delete an existing style:

1. **Drag the style you wish to delete down to the trash can icon at the bottom of the Styles palette (Figure 12).**

   When you release the mouse button, a dialog box (Figure 13) asks you to confirm its deletion.

2. **Click the OK button.**

   The style is removed from the list.

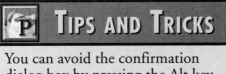

TIPS AND TRICKS

You can avoid the confirmation dialog box by pressing the Alt key when you drag the style into the trash can.

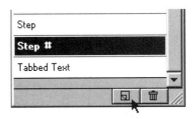

Figure 10. Drag a style to the New Style icon to duplicate it.

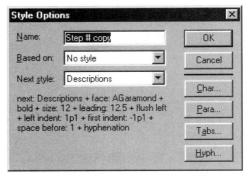

Figure 11. In the Style Options dialog box, rename your style.

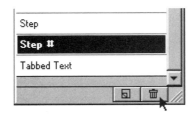

Figure 12. Delete a style by dragging it to the trash can.

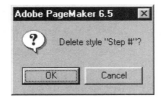

Figure 13. The Delete Confirmation dialog box (just click OK to delete the style).

Figure 14. Double-click on the style.

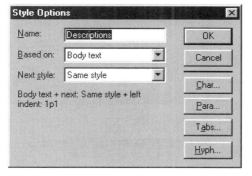

Figure 15. The Style Options dialog box.

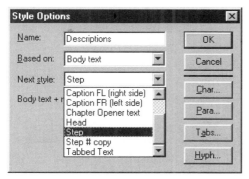

Figure 16. Choose the style to cascade to from the Next style pop-up menu.

Cascading styles

Another powerful capability of styles is the ability to switch to another style when you press Return. In this way you can set up a series of styles to be applied automatically as you type within PageMaker.

I used cascading styles when creating this book. For most of the steps, I typically have a heading followed by a numbered step, followed by a description of that step, followed by another numbered step, followed by a description, etc. So my "Head" style cascades to my "Step #" style, which cascades to my "Description" style, which cascades to my "Step #" style. The Description/Step series continues until I manually change styles. Note this process in the steps below.

To set up cascading style sheets:

1. **Double-click on the style you wish to cascade *from* (Figure 14).**

   The Style Options dialog box for that style appears (**Figure 15**).

2. **From the Next style pop-up menu, select the style you wish to cascade *to* (Figure 16).**

   Now when you press a Return while in the "from" style, the next paragraph will automatically become the "to" style.

3. **Click the OK button.**

   The style is now set to cascade to the next style.

Automating Style Changes by Cascading Styles

The Based on Style feature

The Based on option in the Style Options dialog box allows you to base a style on another style. Besides the apparent benefit of ensuring that styles have similar attributes, the Based on feature allows you to make changes to several styles at once.

Here's how it works: Let's say that my Body text style (what the main type is styled as) is the first style I create. The next style I create is the Step # style, which is bold, and has a certain indenting. If I base Step # on Body Text, changes I make to Body Text will affect Step #. For instance, if my publisher said "Ted, you can't use Lefty Casual as your font," I could just change the font of the Body Text style, and all other styles (including Step #) would change to a different font automatically. This could allow me, in theory, to make document-wide changes with just a few clicks.

To base a style on another style:

1. **Double-click the style you want to base on another style (Figure 17).**

   The Style Options dialog box appears (**Figure 18**).

2. **Choose a style from the Based on pop-up menu and click OK (Figure 19).**

   The first style is now based on the style you chose in the pop-up menu. Any changes to the based-on style will be reflected in the style you just modified.

Figure 17. Double-click on the style.

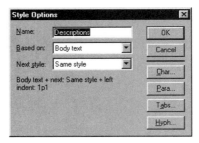

Figure 18. The Style Options dialog box.

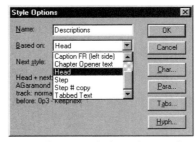

Figure 19. Choose a style from the Based on pop-up menu.

TIPS AND TRICKS

It is a good idea to make your original style (the one everything else is based on) standard text, such as body copy, and *not* a headline, a caption, or some other strongly-formatted text.

Mimicking Styles

Figure 20. Double-click on the style.

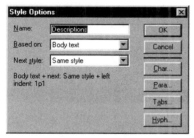

Figure 21. The Style Options dialog box.

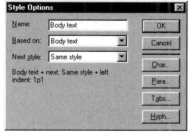

Figure 22. Type in the name of the style you want to merge with.

Figure 23. The Replace Confirmation dialog box.

Merging styles

You can "merge" two different styles together in PageMaker, to help keep your document more organized and less cluttered. In this way you can automatically make all text that is one style another style instantly.

For instance, if I was using a style called "Body Copy" and another style called "Basic Text," and I wanted both styles to have the same attributes as Body Copy, I would merge Basic Text with Body Copy, keeping only the Body Copy style. All the text that had formerly been Basic Text would then be Body Copy from that point forward.

To merge two styles:

1. **Double-click the style that contains the attributes you want to use for the text from both styles (Figure 20).**

   The Style Options dialog box appears (**Figure 21**).

   If both styles have the same attributes (and you're *sure* of this), it doesn't matter which one you double-click on.

2. **Rename the style exactly the same name as the style you want to merge it with and click the OK button (Figure 22).**

   A dialog box will ask if you really want to replace that style (**Figure 23**).

3. **Click the OK button.**

   The styles will be combined into the newly-named style.

Merging Styles

Using styles from other documents

You can use styles that were created in other PageMaker documents by importing just the styles into your current document.

To import styles from other PageMaker documents:

1. **Choose Type⇨Define Styles (Ctrl+3) (Figure 24).**

   The Define Styles dialog box appears (**Figure 25**).

2. **Click the Import button.**

   A dialog box appears allowing you to choose the file from which to import styles (**Figure 26**).

3. **Select the file and click OK.**

   If the file you selected has styles that are in use in the current document, a warning dialog box appears asking if you want to overwrite styles (**Figure 27**).

   Clicking the OK button will import the styles from the document you selected, redefining styles in your current document with the same name. Be careful when doing this, as there is no way to undo a redefined style.

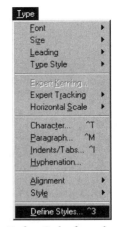

Figure 24. Choose Define Styles from the Type menu.

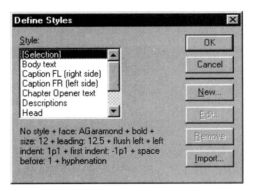

Figure 25. The Define Styles dialog box.

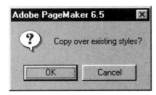

Figure 27. The warning that appears when you attempt to import styles that are already in the current document.

Figure 26. Choose the file which contains the styles you wish to import in the Import styles dialog box.

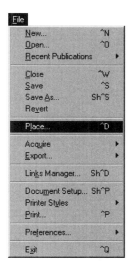

Figure 28. Placed text will automatically import any styles already within that text.

Importing styles when placing text

When you bring styled text into PageMaker, those styles are added to your list of styles.

You can bring text that retains its style into PageMaker in a number of ways:

- Place text via the File⇨Place Command (**Figure 28**).

- Paste text into a text block

- Drag text into a document from another document.

Of course, this is a way to quickly transfer styles between two open PageMaker documents; just drag and drop a text block with the styles in it from one document to another. The styles from the first document appear in the second one.

Styles with the same name are indicated by an asterisk after the style name; that way the original style isn't overwritten. You can always merge similar styles to reduce the number of styles in a document, as described on page 131.

GRAPHICS

PageMaker includes several drawing tools which comprise a good chunk of the toolbox. These tools can be used for simple tasks, such as creating background screens, or more complex touches, such as creating special graphical elements including stars and polygons.

Each of the objects that is created in PageMaker can be modified, edited, and filled and stroked with any color.

This chapter takes you on a tour of PageMaker's drawing tools.

Introduction to Drawing

Drawing in PageMaker

Shapes and lines can be drawn in PageMaker using the drawing tools in the PageMaker toolbox (**Figure 1**). In addition, each of the tools has specific options which can be modified before you draw by double-clicking on the tools. **Figure 2** shows the options for the Polygon tool.

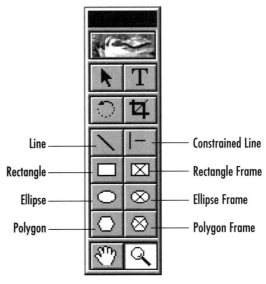

Figure 1. *The shape and line tools in PageMaker.*

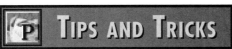

Whenever you create a shape in PageMaker, "sizing handles" appear on the edges and corners of that shape (while it is selected). Dragging a sizing handle on the edge of a shape makes that shape longer or shorter in that direction. Dragging a corner sizing handle changes both the width and height of the shape at the same time.

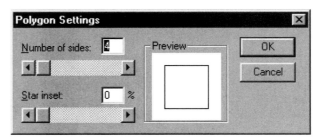

Figure 2. *The Polygon Settings dialog box, which appears when you double-click the Polygon tool.*

Figure 3. The cursor that appears when you select the Rectangle tool.

Figure 4. Click and drag with the Rectangle tool to draw a rectangle.

Figure 5. When you release the mouse button, the rectangle appears in your document.

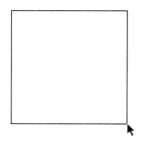

Figure 6. Press the Shift key while dragging to create a square.

To draw a rectangle:

1. **Choose the Rectangle tool from the toolbox.**

   The cursor will change into a little crosshair (**Figure 3**).

2. **Click and drag anywhere on the screen.**

   As you drag, you'll see a rectangle being formed behind the cursor (**Figure 4**).

3. **Release the mouse button when the rectangle is the correct size.**

   A rectangle will appear when you release the mouse button (**Figure 5**).

   If you drag outside the edge of the page, the document will scroll to allow you to extend the rectangle "off" the screen.

To draw a square:

Follow the same steps listed above, but press the Shift key while dragging (Figure 6).

Make sure you keep the Shift key pressed when you release the mouse button; if you release the Shift key first, the square will change to a rectangle.

Drawing Rectangles and Squares

To draw a rounded corner rectangle:

1. **Double-click on the Rectangle tool in the toolbox.**

   The Rounded Corners dialog box appears (**Figure 7**).

2. **Choose a corner setting from the six presets.**

   Rectangles with each of the presets from the Rounded Corners dialog box are shown in **Figure 8**.

3. **Click and drag anywhere on the screen.**

4. **Release the mouse button when the rectangle is the desired size.**

   Pressing the Shift key while drawing a rounded corner rectangle will adjust the height and width of the rectangle so that they are equal.

To draw an ellipse:

1. **Choose the Ellipse tool from the toolbox.**

2. **Click and drag anywhere on the screen.**

   As you drag, you'll see an ellipse being formed behind the cursor (**Figure 9**).

3. **Release the mouse button when the ellipse is the desired size.**

   The ellipse appears in your document with sizing handles (**Figure 10**).

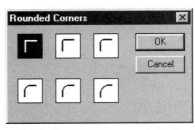

Figure 7. The Rounded Corners dialog box.

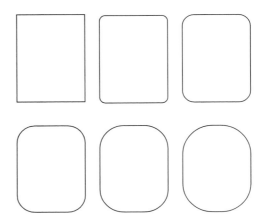

Figure 8. Each of the six rounded rectangles.

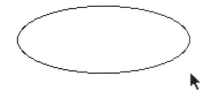

Figure 9. An ellipse in the process of being drawn.

Figure 10. A completed ellipse, with sizing handles shown.

Drawing Ellipses and Rounded Corner Rectangles

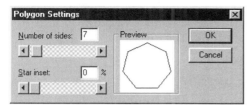

Figure 11. The Polygon Settings dialog box.

Figure 12. A seven-sided polygon with control handles showing.

Figure 13. Click on each point to manually draw a polygon.

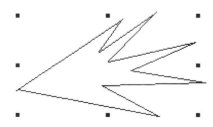

Figure 14. A manually drawn polygon.

To automatically draw a polygon:

1. **Double-click on the Polygon tool in the toolbox.**

   The Polygon Settings dialog box appears (**Figure 11**).

2. **Drag the top slider or enter the number of sides and click OK.**

   Enter any number between 3 and 100. The upper limit is 100 because at that point, you might as well just draw a circle by pressing Shift while drawing an ellipse.

3. **Click and drag anywhere on the screen.**

   A polygon will appear as you draw.

4. **Release the mouse button when the polygon is the correct size (Figure 12).**

   Pressing the Shift key while drawing a polygon will constrain all sides of the polygon so that they are equal.

To manually draw a polygon:

1. **Click on the Polygon tool in the toolbox.**

2. **Click (don't drag) on your document.**

   A point appears.

3. **Move the cursor and click again.**

   A line appears between the two points (**Figure 13**).

4. **Continue clicking until you close the object (Figure 14).**

To draw a star:

1. **Double-click on the Polygon tool in the toolbox.**

   The Polygon Settings dialog box appears (**Figure 15**).

2. **Set the number of sides by dragging the Number of sides slider or by typing in a specific number.**

   This setting is really the number of points on the star.

3. **Increase the Star inset value.**

   The Star inset value "breaks" polygon sides in the middle, pulling them inward.

4. **Click the OK button.**

   The Polygon Settings dialog box closes.

5. **Click and drag in your document to create a star (Figure 16).**

   Pressing the Shift key while drawing a star will constrain all sides of the polygon so that they are equal (**Figure 17**).

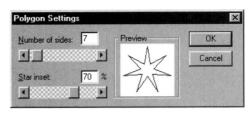

Figure 15. The Polygon Settings dialog box, set to create stars instead of standard polygons.

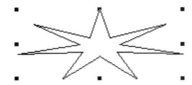

Figure 16. A star with control handles showing.

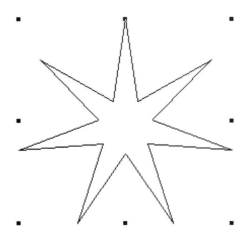

Figure 17. A star drawn while the Shift key was pressed.

Drawing Stars

Figure 18. Click on the object you wish to resize.

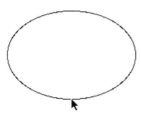

Figure 19. Dragging the handle in the bottom center of the object changes only its height.

To change the size of an existing object:

1. Choose the Pointer tool in the toolbox.

2. Click on the object you wish to resize (**Figure 18**).

   The sizing handles appear around the object.

3. Click on any one of the sizing handles and drag (**Figure 19**).

   Figure 20 shows the function of each sizing handle.

Changing the Size of Objects

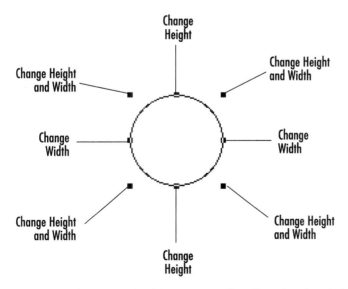

Figure 20. How dragging each of the sizing handles affects the selected object.

143

Default fills and strokes

PageMaker can fill and stroke any of its objects with a variety of different fill and stroke patterns. In addition, each of these patterns and fills can be colored and tinted in any way you like (coloring and tinting is discussed in detail in Chapter 14).

To choose a default fill:

1. **With the Pointer tool, select the object(s) you want to modify.**

2. **Choose Element ⇨ Fill ⇨ and the pattern you wish to use.**

   The Fill submenu is shown in **Figure 21.**

   The object(s) are filled with the pattern you chose.

   If no object is selected, choosing a different default fill affects all new objects created in that document.

To choose a default stroke:

1. **With the Pointer tool, select the object(s) which requires a new (or different) stroke.**

   If no object is selected, choosing a different default stroke affects all new objects created in that document.

2. **Choose Element ⇨ Stroke ⇨ and the pattern you wish to use.**

   The Stroke submenu is shown in **Figure 22.**

***Figure 21.** The Fill submenu.*

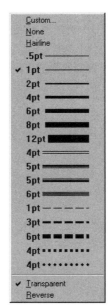

***Figure 22.** The Stroke submenu.*

TIPS AND TRICKS

A *fill* is considered to be the inside area of any object. A *stroke* is the line that surrounds the object. Each object can have only one fill and one stroke.

Default Fills and Strokes

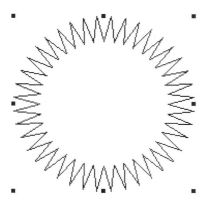

Figure 23. The object must be selected before changes can be made to it.

Figure 24. Choose Fill and Stroke from the Element menu.

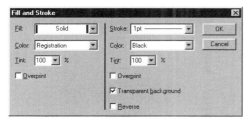

Figure 25. The Fill and Stroke dialog box.

To modify fill and stroke at the same time:

1. **With the Pointer tool, select the object(s) you wish to modify (Figure 23).**

   If no object is selected, changing the fill and stroke affects all new objects created in that document.

2. **Choose Element ⇨ Fill and Stroke (Ctrl+U) (Figure 24).**

   The Fill and Stroke dialog box appears (**Figure 25**).

3. **Choose from the myriad of options in the Fill and Stroke dialog box, then click OK.**

   The object will be filled and stroked with the fill and stroke chosen in that box (**Figure 26**).

Figure 26. After applying the fill and stroke changes to the selected object.

Fill and Stroke Design

Creating lines in PageMaker

Did I mention before that the PageMaker toolbox has one of the most useless tools in the world? No, it never had a "Zoom to Current Magnification" tool. Instead, it has something equally useless: the Constrained Line tool. Why is it useless? Because by holding down the Shift key with the Line tool, you get *exactly* the same results. But maybe it just *looks* nice next to the Line tool. Hmmm.

Figure 27. Select the Line tool from the toolbox.

To create a line in PageMaker:

1. Select the Line tool from the toolbox (**Figure 27**).

2. Click and drag on the document to draw your line.

   As you drag, a line will appear (**Figure 28**).

Figure 28. Click and drag to draw a line.

3. Release the mouse button, and the line will be drawn and selected, with sizing handles on either end.

   Press the Shift key while drawing (and keep it pressed until after you release the mouse button) to angle the line in increments of 45°.

Figure 29. Click on a line with the Pointer tool in order to resize it.

To resize an existing line:

1. Click on a line with the Pointer tool.

   Two sizing handles will appear (**Figure 29**).

2. Click on either sizing handle and drag (**Figure 30**).

Figure 30. Click and drag on one of the sizing handles at each end of the line to change the direction and length of the line.

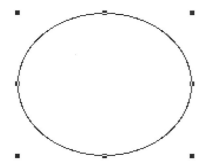

Figure 31. Select the object to which you want to apply a custom stroke.

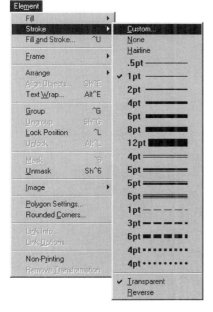

Figure 32. Choose Custom from the Stroke submenu in the Element menu.

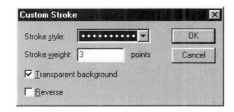

Figure 33. The Custom Stroke dialog box.

Custom strokes

In addition to the default stroke settings (selected from either the Stroke submenu or from the Fill and Stroke dialog box), there are also custom stroke settings which you can define.

To create a custom stroke:

1. **Select the object whose stroke you wish to customize (Figure 31).**

   If no object is selected, the changes will affect all strokes created after the custom stroke setting has been defined.

2. **Choose Element ⇨ Stroke ⇨ Custom (Figure 32).**

   The Custom Stroke dialog box will appear (**Figure 33**).

3. **Make any adjustments you want within the Custom Stroke dialog box and click OK.**

4. **The selected object's stroke will match the settings in the Custom Stroke dialog box (Figure 34).**

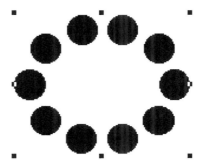

Figure 34. After the settings from the Custom Stroke dialog box have been applied to the selected object.

Customizing Strokes

147

Fill and stroke examples

So you might get a better idea of how fill and stroke work, this page contains example objects (**Figures 35-38**) that have different fills and strokes applied to them.

Figure 35. This rectangle has a 4 pt. dotted black stroke and a diagonal line pattern fill.

Figure 37. This "tube" was created by placing several circles on top of one another, and changing the fill for each of them, while leaving the stroke at 2 pt. black.

Figure 36. This image consists of three overlapping stars. The backmost one has a 2 pt. black stroke and a 65% black fill. The middle one has no stroke and a 25% black fill. The front star has no stroke and a white fill.

Figure 38. The "pattern" for this object really isn't a pattern at all. Instead, white four-pointed stars were placed on the gray ellipse to simulate a pattern.

PLACING IMAGES

Documents take on an entirely new dimension when images, both photographs and other artwork, are placed into them. PageMaker excels in this area; it works seamlessly with other Adobe products such as Photoshop and Illustrator.

Once graphics are in place, PageMaker allows you to crop, size, and even colorize these placed images.

To place an image into a PageMaker document:

1. **Open the document and move to the page on which you wish to place the image.**

   Actually, you can be on a different page, and then click on the page you want to go to using the page icons at the bottom, but it's easier if you're already on the correct page.

2. **Choose the Pointer tool from the toolbox.**

   If you have chosen the Text tool and are in a text block, the graphic will appear as an inline graphic—a graphic that is part of a text block that flows along with text.

3. **Choose File ⇨ Place (Ctrl+D) (Figure 1).**

   The Place dialog box appears (**Figure 2**).

4. **Locate the image you wish to place and click OK.**

   The cursor changes to the Place cursor (**Figure 3**).

5. **Click anywhere in the document.**

   The image appears (at actual size) in the document (**Figure 4**).

   The image can be resized using the sizing handles (see the following page).

Figure 1. Choose Place from the File menu.

Figure 2. The Place dialog box.

Figure 3. The Place cursor.

Figure 4. An image after being placed.

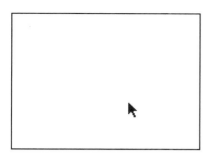

Figure 5. Dragging a placed image shows an outline of the entire image.

Figure 6. The sizing handles on a placed image.

To move a placed image:

1. Choose the Pointer tool from the toolbox.

2. Click on the image you wish to move and drag it to a new location.

   As you drag, an outline of the image area (always a rectangle) will appear under your cursor (**Figure 5**).

3. When the image is in the location you want, release the mouse button.

   The image will appear in the new location.

P TIPS AND TRICKS

If you click *and hold* for a second before moving the mouse, a "ghost" image of the placed art will be moved, not just an outline.

To resize a placed image:

1. Choose the Pointer tool from the toolbox.

2. Click on the object you wish to resize.

   Sizing handles will appear around the object (**Figure 6**).

3. Click and drag on any of the sizing handles to adjust the size of the image.

P TIPS AND TRICKS

Pressing the Shift key while resizing constrains the placed image to its original proportions. Remember to keep pressing the Shift key until after you release the mouse button; otherwise the object's proportions may not match its original shape.

Moving and Resizing Placed Images

To link, or to embed?

When you place an image in PageMaker, you're given the choice to either link or embed the image you're selecting.

Linking an image puts a proxy of the image in your PageMaker document. It lets you see that image onscreen, on the page. You can crop, resize, move, and rotate the image, but the original image is unaffected in another location on your hard drive. The original image file must accompany the PageMaker document when you give the PageMaker file to someone else to print or modify.

Embedding an image makes that image a part of the PageMaker document. Embedded images can be modified by moving, scaling, rotating, and cropping.

Typically, images are linked to PageMaker documents, and not embedded. In fact, you have to go through a few hoops to embed an image, while linking an image is almost mindless (the simple act of placing an image automatically links it by default). Each image that is embedded in a PageMaker document makes the document larger by the size of the placed image, while linked images take up only a fraction of that size.

I try to store all the image files from each PageMaker document I create in the same folder as the original PageMaker document. For this book, each chapter is a document, and I created a separate folder for each document. **Figure 7** shows the files from one of the larger chapters of the book.

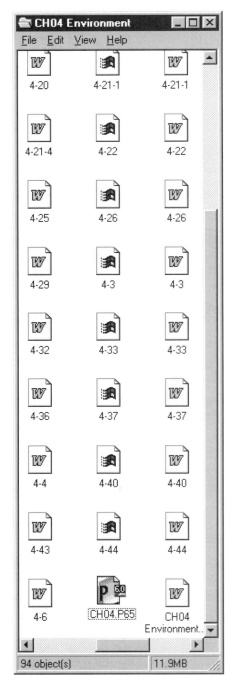

Figure 7. A window containing a PageMaker document and placed files.

Figure 8. Choose Links Manager from the File menu.

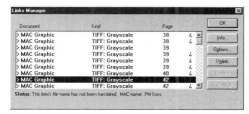

Figure 9. The Links Manager dialog box.

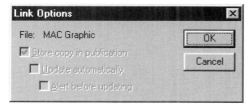

Figure 10. The Link Options dialog box.

To embed an image:

1. Place an image into your document as described on page 150.

2. Choose File ➪ Links Manager (Ctrl+Shift+D) (**Figure 8**).

   The Links Manager dialog box appears (**Figure 9**).

3. Select the name of the image you wish to embed by clicking on it.

4. Click the Options button.

   The Link Options dialog box appears (**Figure 10**).

5. Click the Store copy in publication checkbox.

6. Click the OK button in each dialog box.

   The placed image is now embedded within the PageMaker document.

TIPS AND TRICKS

If you don't select an image when clicking the Options button in the Links Manager dialog box, the changes you make will affect all future placed images. If you check the Store copy in publication checkbox before you place any image, you'll automatically embed each image you place. Be aware that embedding an image can give even a small document a humongous file size.

Embedding an Image

153

PageMaker's placed image file formats

PageMaker supports several file formats for placed images. File types include:

- PICT
- TIFF
- EPS
- GIF
- WMF (Windows)
- EMF (Windows)

There are two main *types* of graphics that can be placed into PageMaker: pixel-based art and vector-based art.

Pixel-based art (**Figure 11**) is created from thousands of pixels (little colored squares) in each image, which, when viewed together, resemble a shape, an object, a person, a landscape, etc. Photographs are always pixel-based images. Pixel-based artwork is generated by scanners and software such as Adobe Photoshop and Painter.

Vector-based artwork (**Figure 12**) is created from several colored "shapes," which can resemble almost anything. Vector artwork is used for logos, illustrations, and typography. Vectors are created by applications such as Adobe Illustrator. An advantage to using vectors is that they can be resized without any loss of quality. While pixel-based art can be any of the file types listed above, vector-based artwork can only be PICT or EPS.

Figure 11. A pixel-based image.

Figure 12. A vector-based image.

File Formats

Figure 13. The left side of this image (Pyro) is shown with Standard graphics display, while the right half (Linus T.) is shown in high resolution.

Figure 14. The same image after choosing the Gray out option.

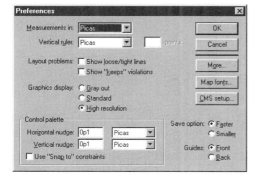

Figure 15. The Preferences dialog box. The center of the dialog box contains the three Graphics display options.

Graphics display options

PageMaker can display graphics that are placed in documents in three different ways:

Standard means that the graphic appears at screen resolution, which looks great until you zoom in on an image (**Figure 13**).

High resolution looks the same as Standard at 100%, but once you zoom in, the image retains its quality (**Figure 13**). The High resolution setting slows down PageMaker dramatically if many images are placed in the document.

Gray out makes all images that are not selected grayed out, providing previews that are extremely zippy, and bearable on even slower computers (**Figure 14**).

To change the graphics display options:

1. **Choose File ⇨ Preferences ⇨ General (Ctrl+K)**

   The Preferences dialog box appears (**Figure 15**).

2. **Choose a Graphics display option from the three settings.**

3. **Click the OK button.**

   All graphics in the document will be affected by the change.

Graphics Display Options

Modifying images within PageMaker

PageMaker provides several ways to modify placed images. Grayscale images can be colorized (see Chapter 14) and drastically changed in appearance with the Image Control feature.

To modify an image with Image Control:

1. Select the image you wish to modify (**Figure 16**).

2. Choose Element ⇨ Image ⇨ Image Control.

   The Image Control dialog box appears (**Figure 17**).

3. Make any adjustments to the Image Control dialog box (**Figure 18**).

   The image in the Tips and Tricks below was brightened, and the Contrast was reduced.

4. Click OK.

   The image will reflect the changes you've made (**Figure 19**).

TIPS AND TRICKS

You can create a nifty screened background (like the one behind this text) by lightening an image and placing it behind text. Be sure to lighten the image enough so that the words are readable on the background. In some cases, you might want to use **bold** for text that uses a faded image as a background.

Figure 16. Select the image you wish to modify.

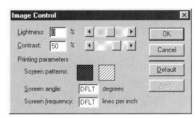

Figure 17. The Image Control dialog box.

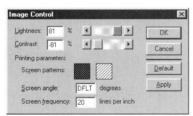

Figure 18. After making changes to the Image Control dialog box.

Figure 19. The resulting image.

Image Control

Besides being able to place graphics anywhere in a document, PageMaker has the ability to place a graphic within a text block. The advantage to doing this (as opposed to just placing it in any location) is that the graphic then flows along with the text, so edits and revisions to the text move the graphic automatically.

Figure 20. Click in the text block where you'd like the graphic to appear.

Besides being able to place graphics anywhere in a document, PageMaker has the ability to place a graphic within a text block. ⭐ The advantage to doing this (as opposed to just placing it in any location) is that the graphic then flows along with the text, so edits and revisions to the text move the graphic automatically.

Figure 21. The graphic appears in the text block.

Inline Graphics

Besides being able to place graphics anywhere in a document, PageMaker has the ability to place a graphic within a text block—this is called an inline graphic. The advantage to this (as opposed to just placing it in any location) is that the graphic then flows along with the text, so edits and revisions to the text cause the graphic to move automatically.

To create an inline graphic:

1. **Place your cursor in a text block where you'd like the graphic to appear (Figure 20).**

2. **Choose File ⇨ Place.**
   The Place dialog box appears.

3. **Locate and select the file you wish to use as an inline graphic, then click OK.**
   The graphic will appear in the text block (**Figure 21**).

   Artwork used as inline graphics can be deleted by clicking to the right of them with the Text tool and then pressing the Backspace key.

Creating Inline Graphics

Adobe's desktop publishing trio is one part PageMaker, one part Photoshop, and one part Illustrator. Together, they offer limitless possibilities to what you can produce on your computer.

Adobe has given this troika of programs as common an interface as possible, from the toolbox to the menus to the keyboard commands. There's still quite a ways to go, but with the current (as of this writing) set of programs, specifically Adobe PageMaker 6.5, Adobe Illustrator 7.0, and Adobe Photoshop 4.0, there is much more alike than different.

This chapter explores exchanging files between these programs, as well as providing some basics about Illustrator and Photoshop.

Introduction to Photoshop and Illustrator

From Photoshop to PageMaker

There are several ways to bring images from Photoshop into PageMaker. The most common method is to save a Photoshop document in a format that can be placed by PageMaker. This allows both linked and embedded graphics. But there are two other, much quicker, methods that result in embedded graphics: copying from Photoshop and pasting into PageMaker, and dragging from Photoshop into PageMaker.

To paste an image from Photoshop into PageMaker:

1. In Photoshop, select the image (or portion of an image) you wish to copy (**Figure 1**).

   You can use any selection method and tool for your selection.

2. In Photoshop, choose Edit⇨Copy (Ctrl+C) (**Figure 2**).

3. In PageMaker, choose Edit⇨Paste (Ctrl+V).

   The image appears in your PageMaker document (**Figure 3**).

To drag an image from Photoshop into PageMaker:

1. In Photoshop, select the image you wish to copy.

2. Press the Ctrl key and drag from the Photoshop window to the PageMaker window.

   The image will appear in PageMaker.

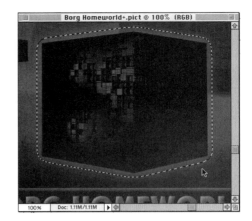

Figure 1. Select an image in Photoshop.

Figure 2. Choose Copy from the Edit menu.

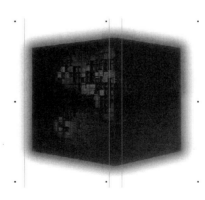

Figure 3. And paste into PageMaker.

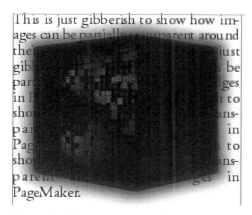

This is just gibberish to show how images can be partially transparent around the [...] just gibberish [...] be partially [...] ges in [...] to show [...] ans-parent [...] in PageMaker [...] to show [...] ans-parent [...] in PageMaker.

Figure 4. This image is partially transparent at the edges, showing the text behind the image.

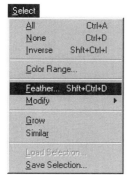

Figure 5. Choose Feather from the Select menu.

Figure 6. In the Feather Selection dialog box, enter the width of the feathering.

Cool stuff you can do with Photoshop images

Photoshop's feathering capabilities are wonderful, but they're even better when they are used in PageMaker. Any Photoshop image that you paste/drop into PageMaker can be *partially transparent,* as shown in **Figure 4.**

To make the edges of an image partially transparent:

1. **In Photoshop, make your selection.**

2. **Choose Select⇨Feather (Figure 5).**
   The Feather Selection dialog box appears (**Figure 6**).

3. **Enter the amount of feathering you want for the image, in pixels, and click OK.**
   The higher the number in the Feather Radius field, the "fuzzier" or more "see through" the edge will be.

4. **Copy/drag from Photoshop and paste/drop into PageMaker.**
   The transparency remains!

Using "partial" selections like this—where some pixels are partially selected—allows you to create all sorts of interesting effects without going to the trouble of creating a Photoshop clipping path.

The Photoshop environment

Working in Photoshop is very much like working in PageMaker. That was Adobe's goal: to make the interfaces of their major products work and feel the same. The Photoshop environment is shown in **Figure** 7.

Photoshop's Filter Menu

The Filter menu in Photoshop is used for applying all sorts of effects to images. Some of these filters are available in PageMaker (see Chapter 13).

Photoshop's Menu Bar

The menu bar contains most of Photoshop's commands. Many keyboard commands (Like Ctrl+1 for 100% view) are common to both programs.

Photoshop's Toolbox

The toolbox includes tools for selecting images, drawing and painting, modifying images, and changing colors. It bears a strong resemblance to the PageMaker toolbox.

Photoshop's Status bar

The Status bar along the bottom left of the document window shows the current zoom level and Photoshop's efficiency (the lower the number, the more it is using your hard drive for a swap file).

Figure 7. The Photoshop environment.

Photoshop's Title Bar

The title bar of each document not only contains the name of that document, but also the viewing percentage (in this case 300%), and the color mode (RGB).

Photoshop's Palettes

All of Photoshop's palettes use tabs, just like PageMaker's. The Layers palette (hidden in the top palette) is very much like PageMaker's Layers palette.

Photoshop's Channels

The Channels palette contains a different channel for each color in the image (three for RGB, four for CMYK), and additional channels for masking.

Photoshop's Navigator

The Navigator palette allows you to zip around your Photoshop document without scrolling. Just click in the area you would like to view, and the main screen is redrawn.

Photoshop's Swatches

The Swatches palette contains a selection of different colors to choose from while working in Photoshop. There are different Swatch palettes available.

The Photoshop Environment

From Illustrator to PageMaker

As with Photoshop, there are several ways to transfer images from Illustrator into PageMaker. The most common way is to save an Illustrator document in a format that can be placed by PageMaker. This allows both linked and embedded graphics. But there are two other, much quicker, methods that result in embedded graphics: copying from Illustrator and pasting into PageMaker, and dragging from Illustrator into PageMaker.

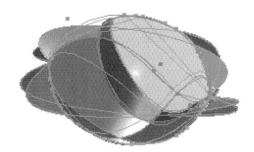

Figure 8. Select the art in Illustrator.

To paste an image from Illustrator into PageMaker:

1. **In Illustrator, select the image (or pieces of an image) you wish to copy (Figure 8).**

   Only objects that are selected can be copied and pasted.

2. **In Illustrator, choose Edit⇨Copy (Ctrl+C) (Figure 9).**

Figure 9. Choose Copy from the Edit menu.

3. **In PageMaker, choose Edit⇨Paste (Ctrl+V).**

   The image will appear in your PageMaker document (**Figure 10**).

To drag an image from Illustrator into PageMaker:

1. **In Illustrator, select the image you wish to copy.**

2. **Using one of Illustrator's selection tools, drag from the Illustrator window to the PageMaker window.**

   The image appears in PageMaker.

Figure 10. After pasting into PageMaker.

Figure 11. Two concentric circles filled with radial gradients.

Figure 12. After making the circles into a compound path with a see-through hole.

Figure 13. After scaling and rotating the ring.

Figure 14. A masking path was drawn to hide the portion of the ring "behind" the ball.

Figure 15. The finished placed EPS image.

Using Illustrator's compound paths and masks

Illustrator allows you to combine vector-based and pixel-based images together to create incredible images. The following example shows just one way to take advantage of Illustrator's capabilities before placing an image in a PageMaker document.

To create a "sports" planet:

1. **In Illustrator, import the image to be used as the planet.**

   I used a basketball for this example.

2. **Create two concentric circles with the Ellipse tool and fill them with a radial gradient (Figure 11).**

   I took the "rainbow" gradient and turned on the Radial option on the Gradient palette.

3. **Select both circles and choose Object ➪ Compound Path ➪ Make (Figure 12).**

4. **Vertically scale the "ring" about 40% and rotate it about 20° (Figure 13).**

5. **Copy the ring.**

6. **Mask out the top section of the ring (Figure 14).**

7. **Paste In Back (Ctrl+B).**

   The final artwork is ready to be selected and brought into PageMaker (**Figure 15**).

Compound Paths and Masks

The Illustrator environment

Working in Illustrator is also very much like working in PageMaker. In fact, Illustrator is even more similar to PageMaker than Photoshop is (**Figure 16**).

Illustrator's Menu Bar

The menu bar contains most of Illustrator's commands. Many keyboard commands (Like Ctrl+1 for 100% view) are common to all three programs.

Illustrator's Toolbox

The toolbox includes tools for selecting images, drawing and painting, transforming, and changing colors. It also bears a resemblance to the PageMaker and Photoshop toolboxes.

Illustrator's Status Bar

The Status bar along the bottom left of the document window shows the current zoom level and a special menu that can show the tool being used, memory, and other information.

Illustrator's Filter Menu

The Filter menu in Illustrator is used for applying both vector and raster filters to images. PageMaker can use Illustrator filters as well as Photoshop filters.

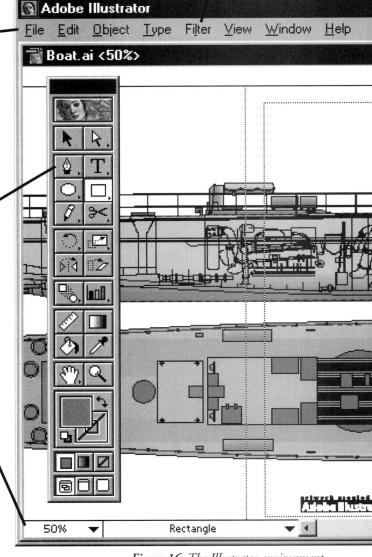

Figure 16. The Illustrator environment.

Illustrator's Title Bar

The title bar of each document not only contains the name of that document, but also the viewing percentage (in this case 50%).

Illustrator's Palettes

All of Illustrator's palettes use tabs, just like PageMaker's, but they're also dockable. The Layers palette (hidden under the Swatches palette) is very much like PageMaker's Layers palette.

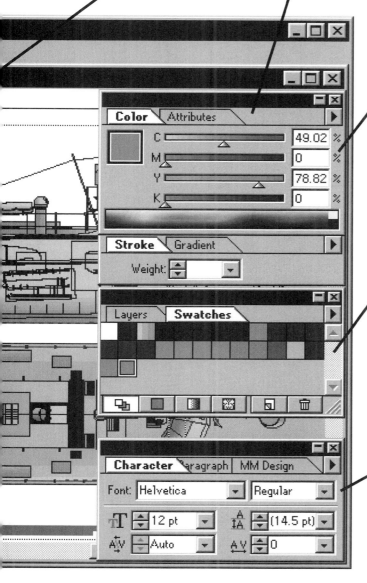

Illustrator's Color palette

The Illustrator Color palette is used for applying different color to object fills and strokes.

Illustrator's Swatches

The Swatches palette contains a selection of different colors to choose from while working in Illustrator. There are different Swatch palettes available.

Illustrator's Character palette

The Character palette is Illustrator's version of PageMaker's Character Attributes Control palette.

The Illustrator Environment

How Illustrator art was used in this book

Each of the chapter opening pages in this book contains a placed Illustrator image as the background. I created the art in Illustrator by using a custom Hatch set, filling a large rectangle with a texture created with the Ink Pen filter.

I had to be sure that the texture was light enough so that it didn't muddy the text in front of it. I placed it in PageMaker (**Figure 17**), and then stretched it so that it would bleed 1/4" around the outside edge of the page. Then the text was placed on top of the image. **Figure 18** shows this chapter's opening page as it appears in PageMaker.

The Illustrator document was fairly complex, so the page does take a bit longer to print than other pages within each chapter.

Figure 17. The texture as it appears in PageMaker as a placed image.

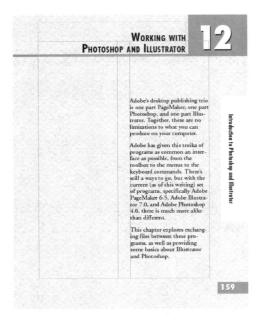

Figure 18. How the chapter opening page appears in PageMaker.

One of the reasons that Photoshop has become virtually the *only* image editing application for professionals is its support for plug-in filters. Plug-in sets such as Kai's Power Tools, Eye Candy, and Extensis PhotoTools have become an industry all their own. Plus, plug-in filters usually do all sorts of cool stuff that Adobe would have loved to stick into Photoshop, if only they weren't so busy making sure it all worked properly.

PageMaker can apply Photoshop filters to placed images through its Photoshop Effects command. This chapter details that process, and the effects of some of the different filters currently available. Some Photoshop filters actually come with PageMaker; others you'll need to purchase separately.

To apply a Photoshop filter to an image within PageMaker:

1. **Place the image in the PageMaker document (Figure 1).**

   If you already have a placed image you'd like to apply the filter to, select that image with the Pointer tool.

2. **Choose Element ⇨ Image ⇨ Photoshop Effects (Figure 2).**

   The Photoshop Effects dialog box appears (**Figure 3**).

3. **Enter a name for the filtered image in the Save new file as text field.**

   PageMaker automatically creates a new linked file when you apply a Photoshop effect to an image.

   If you want to save the file in a location that is different from the original file's location, click the Save As button; this will present you with a standard Save As dialog box.

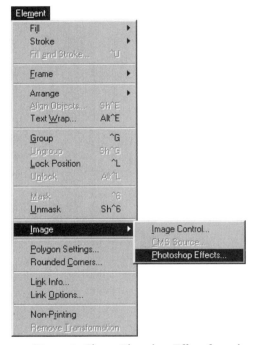

Figure 1. A selected placed image in PageMaker.

Figure 2. Choose Photoshop Effects from the Image submenu in the Element menu.

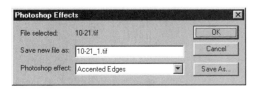

Figure 3. The Photoshop Effects dialog box.

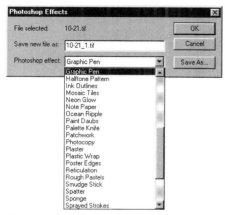

Figure 4. Choose an effect from the pop-up menu.

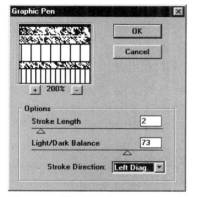

Figure 5. The Graphic Pen Photoshop filter dialog box. Each filter has a slightly different dialog box.

Figure 6. The Graphic Pen effect applied to the image in PageMaker.

4. **From the pop-up menu, choose the Photoshop effect you want to use (Figure 4).**

   All of the Photoshop plug-in filters currently installed in PageMaker will appear in this menu. It may be difficult to find certain filters because the filters are listed alphabetically, regardless of which category they originally appeared in.

5. **Click the OK button.**

   The filter dialog box (if there is one) for the effect you chose will appear (**Figure 5**).

6. **Adjust the controls and values until the preview matches the effect you desire.**

   Some filters do not have previews. Each filter has different controls.

7. **When you've finished adjusting the settings, click the OK button.**

   The effect will be applied to the image (**Figure 6**).

Applying Photoshop Filters within PageMaker

171

PageMaker comes with several Photoshop filters already installed, but you can add additional filters very easily. Many manufacturers have created Photoshop plug-ins that work in PageMaker, such as Kai's Power Tools and Extensis PhotoTools.

To add Photoshop filters to PageMaker:

1. Quit PageMaker.

2. **In Windows, locate your PageMaker directory and double-click on it to open it.**

   A window appears with all your PageMaker files in it (**Figure 7**).

3. **Double-click on the directory called Rsrc.**

   The Rsrc window appears (**Figure 8**).

4. **Double-click on the USenglsh directory.**

   The USenglsh window appears (**Figure 9**). If you have a non-US English version of PageMaker, use the directory that corresponds to your version of PageMaker.

5. **Drag the plug-in (or plug-in folder) into the Plug-ins folder in the Rrsc window.**

6. **Launch PageMaker.**

   The new effects appear in the Photoshop effects pop-up menu in the Photoshop Effects dialog box.

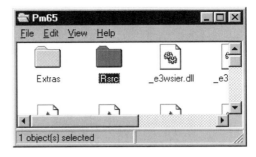

Figure 7. The PageMaker application window.

Figure 8. The Rsrc window.

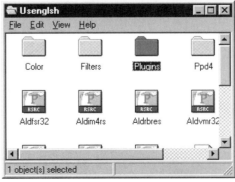

Figure 9. Drag the plug-in (or a folder containing it) into the Plug-ins folder.

Figure 10. The original placed image.

Figure 11. The KPT Page Curl dialog box.

Figure 12. After applying two page curls to the image. Note the strategic placement of the curl along the bottom edge.

Kai's Power Tools

Kai's Power Tools is the most popular plug-in filter set for Photoshop. With more than a dozen effects, you can modify images in all sorts of amazing ways.

To apply KPT Page Curl in PageMaker:

1. **Select the placed image you wish to curl.**

   Figure 10 shows the placed image used in this example.

2. **Choose Element ⇨ Image ⇨ Photoshop Effects.**

   The Photoshop Effects dialog box appears.

3. **Enter a name for the curled image.**

4. **Choose KPT Page Curl from the pop-up menu and click OK.**

   The KPT Page Curl dialog box appears (**Figure 11**).

5. **Click on one of the arrows and drag, then click the green light.**

   The effect is applied to your image.

   I repeated the KPT Page Curl with a different edge for the final effect shown in **Figure 12**.

Using KPT in PageMaker

I created a background texture and placed it behind the text on this page.

To create a background texture with KPT:

1. **Select any image in PageMaker (Figure 13).**

   It doesn't matter what's in the image, just make sure it's big enough to cover the background area.

2. **Choose Element ⇨ Image ⇨ Photoshop Effects.**

   The Photoshop Effects dialog box appears.

3. **Enter a name for the texture.**

4. **Choose KPT Texture Explorer from the pop-up menu and click the OK button.**

   The KPT Texture Explorer dialog box appears (**Figure 14**).

5. **Play with the controls until you have a texture you wish to use.**

6. **Increase the brightness substantially (especially if there will be text in front of the image), then click the checkmark at the lower-right corner of the dialog box.**

   The final background texture is shown behind the text on this page.

Figure 13: Select any placed image. It doesn't matter what's in the image.

Figure 14: The almost indecipherable KPT Texture Explorer dialog box. The current texture is previewed in the center box on the right side.

Figure 15. The original placed image.

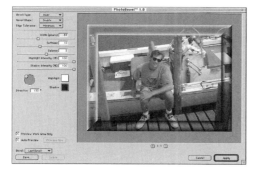

Figure 16. The PhotoBevel dialog box.

Figure 17. After applying the PhotoBevel effect twice, once with a double bevel, and once with a round bevel.

Extensis PhotoTools contains PhotoBevel, a very handy plug-in for making the edges of your photos "pop."

To create an impressive frame with PhotoBevel:

1. **Select the placed image you wish to frame.**

   Figure 15 shows the placed image used in this example.

2. **Choose Element ⇨ Image ⇨ Photoshop Effects.**

   The Photoshop Effects dialog box appears.

3. **Enter a name for the framed image.**

4. **Choose PhotoBevel from the pop-up menu and click OK.**

   The PhotoBevel dialog box appears (**Figure 16**).

5. **Change Bevel Type to Inner and Bevel Shape to Double.**

   You can play with the other settings until you achieve the correct effect.

6. **Click the Apply button.**

   The effect is applied to the image.

7. **Reapply PhotoBevel, but this time use a Round Bevel, with the other settings the same.**

   The final effect is shown in **Figure 17**.

Creating a Picture Frame with PhotoBevel

PageMaker has some pretty incredible color controls and capabilities. Not only can you apply almost any color to any object, but you can also print color separations directly from PageMaker.

CMYK, RGB, and spot colors are supported. This chapter shows you how to use the Colors palette, create new colors, and apply colors to objects.

The Colors palette

The Colors palette (**Figure 1**) is the color nerve center for PageMaker. With it, you can define, apply, and delete colors. You can even modify existing colors.

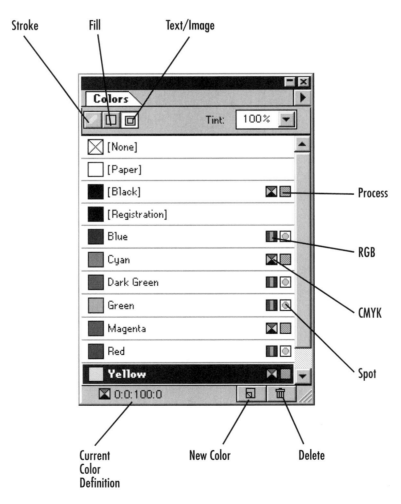

Figure 1. The all-powerful Colors palette.

Color **Me** Magenta

Figure 2. Select the text you wish to color.

Figure 3. Display the Colors palette.

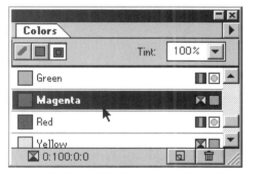

Figure 4. Choose the color in the Colors palette by clicking on it.

Color Me Magenta

Figure 5. The word "Me" after being changed to magenta.

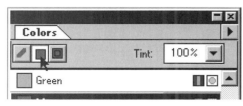

Figure 6. Click the Fill icon in the Colors palette.

To apply a color to text:

1. **Select the text you wish to color (Figure 2).**

   You must use the Type tool to select text.

2. **Display the Colors palette.**

   You can do this by choosing Window⇨Show Colors (**Figure 3**) or by pressing Ctrl+J.

3. **In the Colors palette, click on the color you wish to use for the text (Figure 4).**

   The text changes to the color you've chosen (**Figure 5**).

To apply a color to the fill of a PageMaker object:

1. **Select the object to be changed.**

2. **Display the Colors palette.**

3. **Click the Fill icon in the Colors palette (Figure 6).**

4. **Click on the color you want to use for the fill.**

To apply a color to the stroke of a PageMaker object:

Repeat the steps listed above for changing the fill of an object, but this time click on the Stroke icon instead of the Fill icon in the Colors palette (from Step 3).

The Stroke icon is found to the left of the Fill icon.

Applying Colors

Using None as a color

In PageMaker, you can give an object
a fill or stroke of None. This means
that the fill or stroke will be entirely
transparent.

To apply None as the fill of an object:

1. Select the object you wish to fill
   with None.

2. Display the Colors palette.

3. Click the Fill icon in the Colors
   palette.

4. Click the None option (**Figure 7**).

   The object has a fill of None.

   For **Figure 8**, I used a
   fill of None on the
   ellipse to be used as a
   halo. This allowed the
   background color of
   white and black to
   show through the
   middle of the halo.

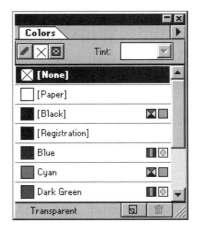

*Figure 7. Choose the None option in the
Colors palette.*

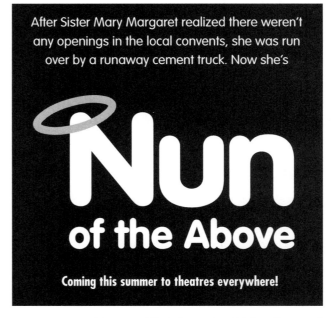

After Sister Mary Margaret realized there weren't
any openings in the local convents, she was run
over by a runaway cement truck. Now she's

Nun

of the Above

Coming this summer to theatres everywhere!

*Figure 8. The halo is a PageMaker ellipse with
a stroke of gray and a fill of None.*

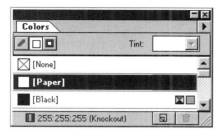

Figure 9. Double-click the Paper color.

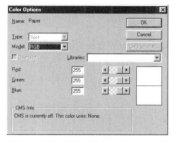

Figure 10. The Color Options dialog box.

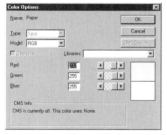

Figure 11. I lowered the Red value to give the page a blue tint.

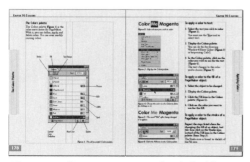

Figure 12. Pages 178-179 with a light blue Paper color.

Paper isn't a color...

One of the odder entries in PageMaker's default color list is Paper, which for the most part is white. The reason that PageMaker calls it Paper instead of White is as follows:

The paper you're using most of the time isn't actually white. It's close, but it isn't the bright white you associate with the screen "white." If you regularly print on newsprint or colored paper, your paper is most definitely something other than white. PageMaker's Paper "color" is the same as whatever you're printing on.

In fact, you can even adjust PageMaker's Paper color to match colored paper if you're printing on a different color than white (see below).

I use the color Paper mostly to cover portions of objects, or to crop objects that can't be cropped otherwise.

To change your paper color:

1. Display the Colors palette.

2. Double-click on the Paper color (**Figure 9**).

   The Color Options dialog box appears (**Figure 10**).

3. Move the Red, Green, and Blue sliders until the color is the correct tint of the paper you'll be using (**Figure 11**).

   Figure 12 shows the previous page spread of this chapter with a light blue Paper color.

The Magic Paper Color

The Color registration

I'll never forget a student I taught a long time ago. She enthusiastically raised her hand when I asked the class if anyone knew what the registration color was.

"It's the official color you use for copyright, trademark, and registered symbols," she said, with no hint of humor in her voice.

"Close..." I said, and somehow managed to explain the following without even cracking a smile.

Registration is a "color" that appears on each printed plate of a document. Crop marks are registration colored. Typically, the registration color is used for marks and notes outside the borders of the printed page—objects which are used by your commercial printer to align colors and trim printed pages.

However, my student did have a good point: by using the registration color on copyright information, you can be sure that regardless of which plates are printed, the copyright information will appear.

To change the color of a PageMaker object to Registration:

1. Select the object you wish to change to Registration.

2. Click on the Fill or Stroke icon in the Colors palette.

3. Click the Registration color in the Colors palette (Figure 13).

    The object will be colored with the Registration color.

Figure 13. Choose Registration from the list of colors in the Colors palette.

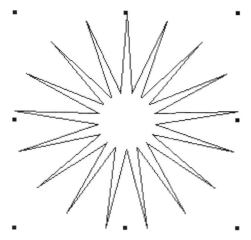

Figure 14. Select an object.

Figure 15. Choose a color in the Colors palette.

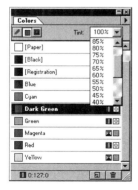

Figure 16. Choose a tint from the pop-up menu.

A tint of a color is a lighter version of that color, defined by a specific percentage—the lower the percentage, the lighter the tint.

To apply a tint of a color to an object:

1. **Select the object that is to have a tinted color applied to it (Figure 14).**

2. **Display the Colors palette.**

3. **Click the Fill or Stroke icon in the Colors palette.**

4. **Click on the color you want to use (Figure 15).**

   By default, the tint value for each selected color is 100%.

5. **Choose a different tint from the Tint pop-up menu (Figure 16).**

   The selected object is tinted (**Figure 17**).

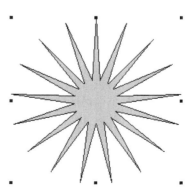

Figure 17. The object after being filled with a 30% tint of Dark Green.

Tinting Colors

183

PageMaker's different color models

When you use a color in PageMaker, you're picking it from a specific color model, whether you're consciously aware of the fact or not. PageMaker has three different color models to choose from:

CMYK: This is the color model to use if you'll be printing your PageMaker document. Commercial printers use cyan (C), magenta (M), yellow (Y), and black (K) inks to create most printable colors. CMYK colors are indicated in the Colors palette by a square with four triangles in it (**Figure 18**).

RGB: Use this color model when creating web pages and onscreen (Acrobat, etc.) documents. Computer monitors use red, green, and blue lights to simulate all the colors that appear on their screens, making it a perfect choice for documents viewed primarily that way. RGB colors are indicated in the Colors palette by a square with three vertical rectangles in it (**Figure 19**).

HLS: Hue, Lightness and Saturation is more of a way of working with colors than it is a color model of its own. I switch to HLS whenever I need to modify one of these specific components, especially Saturation. HLS colors are indicated in the Colors palette by a square with two vertical rectangles: on the left is one that displays hues, and on the right is one that displays a grayscale ramp from white to black (**Figure 20**).

To change the color model of a color:

1. **Double-click the color you wish to change.**

   The Color Options dialog box for that color will appear.

2. **Pick a different color model from the pop-up menu and click the OK button.**

   The color model of that color is changed.

Figure 18. Yellow is a CMYK color, indicated by the square with four triangles in it.

Figure 19. Red is an RGB color, indicated by the square with three vertical rectangles in it.

Figure 20. Turquoisette is an HLS color, indicated by the square with two vertical rectangles in it.

Figure 21. Double-click on the color you wish to change.

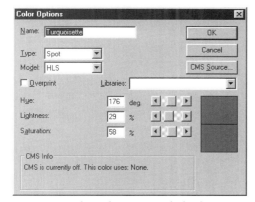

Figure 22. The Color Options dialog box.

Figure 23. Choose Process from the Type pop-up menu.

Figure 24. The top shows the original color as a spot color (note the "spot" icon at the far right), while the bottom shows the color as a process color (where the process icon is now at the far right).

Process colors

Process colors are colors that separate into CMYK color plates when printing. For instance, if you have a color called "Purple" that is 100% cyan, 80% magenta, and 20% yellow, those tints would appear on each separation, respectively.

To make a color a process color:

1. **Double-click the color you wish to change (Figure 21).**

   The Color Options dialog box for that color will appear (**Figure 22**).

2. **Choose Process from the Type pop-up menu (Figure 23) and click the OK button.**

   That color will be changed to a process color (**Figure 24**).

Spot Colors

Spot colors are colors which print on their own exclusive plates. The commercial printer will use a special ink to match that color when printing. In our example from above, the color Purple as a spot color would appear on its own color separation.

To make a color a spot color:

1. **Double-click the color you wish to change.**

   The Color Options dialog box for that color will appear.

2. **Choose Spot from the Type pop-up menu and click OK.**

Pantone™ colors

Pantone colors are special colors, usually used as spot colors, which can be pretty-much guaranteed to match a certain color when printed. Pantone sells a Pantone color book with samples of each spot color for reference. The color you choose on screen will be close to the printed Pantone color, but it won't be exact; such is the nature of the colors that are viewed on screen.

To add a Pantone color to the Colors palette:

1. Display the Colors palette.

2. Click the New Color icon (the little piece of paper next to the trash can) (Figure 25).

   An empty Color Options dialog box appears (with no color defined).

3. Choose Pantone Coated from the Libraries pop-up menu (Figure 26).

   The Color Picker dialog box appears.

4. In the Color Picker, choose the Pantone color you want to use by clicking on it (Figure 27).

5. Click the OK button.

6. Choose either Process or Spot from the Type pop-up menu.

7. Click OK.

   The color is added to the palette.

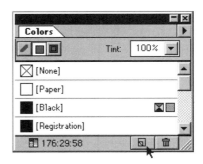

Figure 25. *Click the New Color icon.*

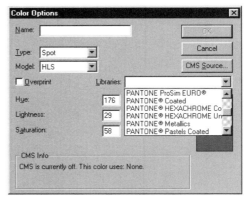

Figure 26. *In the Color Options dialog box, choose a color library from the Libraries pop-up menu.*

Figure 27. *Choose your color in the Color Picker dialog box.*

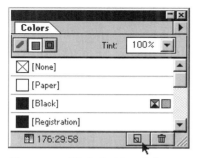

Figure 28. Click the New Color icon.

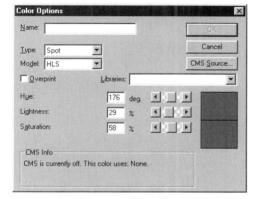

Figure 29. The empty Color Options dialog box appears when you create a new color.

Figure 30. Choose a color type from the Type pop-up menu.

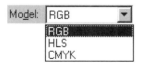

Figure 31. Choose a color model from the Model pop-up menu.

Figure 32. Use a name that is as descriptive as possible when creating new colors...even if you spell it incorrectly.

To create a new color:

1. Display the Colors palette.

2. Click the New Color icon (**Figure 28**).

   An empty Color Options dialog box appears (with no color defined) (**Figure 29**).

3. Choose a color type (**Process or Spot**) from the Type pop-up menu (**Figure 30**).

   The other option, Tint, is discussed on the next page.

4. Choose a color model from the Model pop-up menu (**Figure 31**).

   If the color you want to create already exists in a library, you can also choose a color from the library (described on the previous page).

5. Name your color (**Figure 32**).

   Try to give your color a name that accurately describes it.

6. Define your color values and click the OK button.

   The color will appear in the Colors palette.

To remove a color:

1. Click the color in the Colors palette.

2. Click on the trash can.

   A warning will ask if you're sure you want to get rid of the color; you can avoid this dialog box by pressing Option during this process.

Creating and Removing Colors

187

Color tints

A few pages back, I explained how to tint existing colors. That method works fine for the occasional tinting needs you might have for a small document. But when you're working with a large document that uses tints of 10% and 30% of your spot color, choosing the tint from the Tint pop-up menu gets a little old.

PageMaker allows you to create a tint color from any existing color, to make it easier to apply a tinted color to objects (this way you can quickly apply a color directly from the Colors palette). This tinted color won't print on its own plate, but instead will appear on either its "base" plate or on any CMYK plates its base color uses.

To create a color tint:

1. **Display the Colors palette, then click the New Color icon at the bottom of the Colors palette.**

   The Color Options dialog box appears.

2. **In the Color Options dialog box, choose Tint from the Type pop-up menu (Figure 33).**

   The Model pop-up menu changes to the Base Color pop-up menu.

3. **Choose a base color from the Base Color pop-up menu (Figure 34).**

4. **Choose a Tint value (Figure 35) and name the color tint (Figure 36).**

5. **Click the OK button.**

   The color will be added to the Colors palette.

Figure 33. Choose Tint from the Type pop-up menu in the Color Options dialog box.

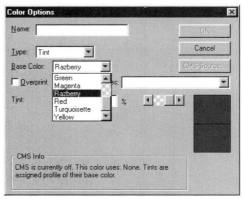

Figure 34. Choose a base color from the Base Color pop-up menu.

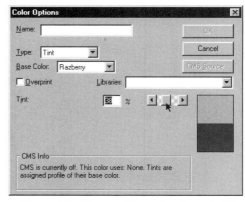

Figure 35. Choose a Tint value from the Tint slider (or type in a value).

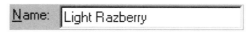

Figure 36. Give the color a descriptive name.

Creating a Color Tint

Figure 37. Double-click on the color you wish to set to overprint.

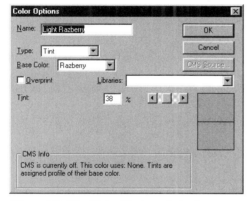

Figure 38. The Color Options dialog box.

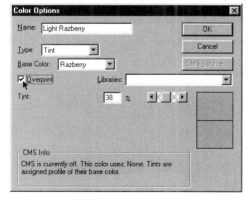

Figure 39. Check the Overprint checkbox.

Overprinting

Colors in PageMaker, by default, knock out any colors underneath them. This works out nicely when you have a yellow oval on a blue background (if the blue is still printed under the yellow, the circle would appear green).

In certain circumstances, like when black text is on top of a tinted background, it is desirable to have the black text overprint the background. PageMaker lets you set colors to overprint using a checkbox in the Color Options dialog box.

To set a color to overprint:

1. **Double-click on the color that you want to set to overprint (Figure 37).**

   The Color Options dialog box for that color appears (**Figure 38**).

2. **Check the Overprint checkbox (Figure 39).**

3. **Click the OK button.**

   That color is set to overprint.

Overprinting

PART IV

LAYOUT

15

Once you venture beyond a single PageMaker page, all sorts of things happen to your document. You can link text from one page to another, or even from one column to another. Text can flow across multiple pages, in any order (it doesn't have to flow from the earlier pages to the later ones).

While this capability of PageMaker can create some intricate documents, editing can be a nightmare in page layout view. PageMaker provides the Story Editor just for this reason. The Story Editor provides a single word-processor-like window for editing the text within a story.

Introduction to Text Flow & the Story Editor

Column guides

Okay. You've set up your document for your newsletter, using all the right margins and such, but something's missing. You want to create a three-column newletter. There are no column breaks on your page. After trying to figure out the math for the width of each column and the space between them, you grab a couple of aspirin and this book. Lucky for you, I'm prepared.

To create column guides:

1. **Open the document in which you want to create column guides.**

   If you don't have any documents open, you can change the column guides setting, and it will affect all *future* documents you create.

2. **Choose Layout ⇨ Column Guides (Figure 1).**

   The Column Guides dialog box appears (**Figure 2**).

3. **Enter the number of columns and space between columns in the text boxes (Figure 3).**

   If you need to set the left pages differently from the right pages, click that checkbox; two additional text boxes will appear (**Figure 4**).

   Usually, you'll need to set left and right pages differently if you're creating a booklet, newsletter, etc.

4. **Click OK.**

   The columns are placed in the document (**Figure 5**).

Figure 1. Choose Column Guides from the Layout menu.

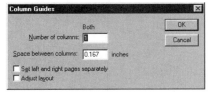

Figure 2. The Column Guides dialog box.

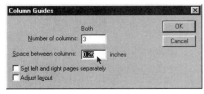

Figure 3. Change the number of columns and space between them.

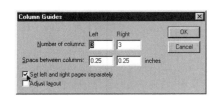

Figure 4. Check the Set left and right pages separately checkbox if necessary.

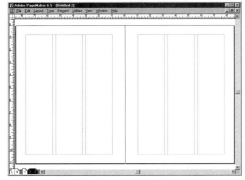

Figure 5. The document with column guides.

Figure 6. The original text columns are uneven after flowing into this page.

Figure 7. I created an additional text block in the rightmost column by shortening the middle column and clicking the down triangle, then clicking in the third column.

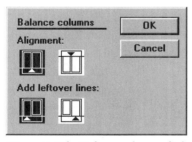

Figure 8. The Balance columns dialog box.

Figure 9. The balanced columns.

Uneven columns

When a story doesn't fill a page that uses multiple columns, the result can be, well, ugly (**Figure 6**). If you want to, you can take the time to shorten the first column and then any remaining columns, but this game gets old and causes even the holiest of men to engage in non-stop cursing. PageMaker has an easier way.

To automatically balance several columns of text:

1. **Using the Pointer tool, link additional text blocks so that there is a text block in each column you wish to fill.**

   For my example, I had to create a text block at the top of the third column (**Figure 7**).

2. **Using the Pointer tool, select all the columns you want to balance.**

3. **Choose Utilities ⇨ Plug-Ins ⇨ Balance Columns.**

   The Balance columns dialog box appears (**Figure 8**).

4. **Choose the way you want your columns to balance by clicking on the appropriate icons, and then click OK.**

   The columns are automatically balanced (**Figure 9**).

   Click the left Alignment icon to make the columns balance along the bottom, and the right one to have them balance along the top.

Autoflow

When you import a large text file into a PageMaker document, it sure would be nice if it just magically flowed throughout the document, filling column after column until the document is stuffed full of text. It would be even nicer if additional pages were added to the document when the current document didn't have enough pages.

Fortunately, PageMaker's Autoflow function does just that. Here's the brief how-to (a more in-depth discussion on this and related issues appears in Chapter 6: Type Objects).

Figure 10. Choose Autoflow from the Layout menu.

To turn on Autoflow:

Choose Layout⇨Autoflow (Figure 10).

If a checkmark appears next to Autoflow, then it is already on (selecting Autoflow from the menu when it is on will turn it off).

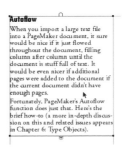

Figure 11. Click on the From text block.

To manually flow text into another column:

1. **With the Pointer tool, click on the text block that currently contains text (Figure 11).**

2. **Click on the little red triangle at the bottom of the text block.**

   Your cursor will change shape, indicating that it is holding text.

   If there's no triangle, you'll need to shorten the text block a bit.

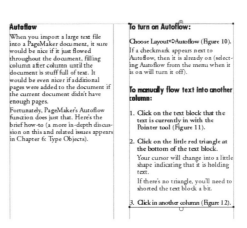

3. **Click in another column (Figure 12).**

   The text flows into that column.

Figure 12. After clicking in another column with the "holding text" cursor.

Autoflow

When you import a large text file into a PageMaker document, it sure would be nice if it just flowed throughout the document, filling column after column until the document is stuff full of text. It would be even nicer if additional pages were added to the document if the current document didn't have enough pages.

Fortunately, PageMaker's Autoflow function does just that. Here's the brief how-to (a more in-depth discussion on this and related issues appears in Chapter 6: Type Objects).

Figure 13. Using the Pointer tool, click on the text block where you want the continued notice.

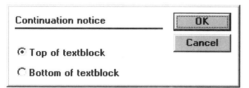

Figure 14. Choose the Bottom of textblock option in the Continuation notice dialog box.

Autoflow

When you import a large text file into a PageMaker document, it sure would be nice if it just flowed throughout the document, filling column after column until the document is stuff full of text. It would be even nicer if additional pages were added to the document if the current document didn't have enough pages.

Fortunately, PageMaker's Autoflow function does just that. Here's the brief how-to (a more in-depth discussion on this and related issues appears in Chapter 6: Type Objects).

Continued on page 197

Figure 15. The continued on notice that appears at the bottom of the original text block.

To add a "continued on" notice to the bottom of a text column:

1. With the Pointer tool, select the text block where you want the "continued on" notice added (**Figure 13**).

2. Choose Utilities ⇨ Plug-ins ⇨ Add Cont'd line.

   The Continuation notice dialog box appears (**Figure 14**).

3. Choose the Bottom of textblock option and click OK.

   A Continued on notice appears in a separate text block under the original text block (**Figure 15**).

   The page number that the text is continued on appears in the box. Be sure that your page numbers are correct *before* you apply this function, as PageMaker does not update page numbers in these boxes automatically.

PageMaker will also place a Continued from notice at the top of the second text block, but you'll have to select that block and choose the Top of textblock option.

P TIPS AND TRICKS

The Continued on notice is created using a style called Cont. On. To get this style to match your text, double-click on it in the Style palette, and set the character attribute to match your body copy + Italics.

The Story Editor

When you have text strewn all through your document, it can be hard to edit; especially when you're moving paragraphs and words from one spot in the story to another. That's where PageMaker's Story Editor comes in.

To use the Story Editor with a single text block:

1. Using the Text tool, click anywhere within a text block (**Figure 16**).

2. Choose Edit ➪ Edit Story. The Story Editor for that text block appears (**Figure 17**).

To use the Story Editor with several text blocks:

1. Using the Pointer tool, select the text blocks you want to view in the Story Editor.

2. Choose Edit ➪ Edit Story. A Story Editor appears for each of the text blocks you've selected (**Figure 18**).

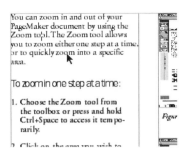

Figure 16. Click in a text block that contains part or all of the story you wish to view in the Story Editor.

Figure 17. The Story Editor for the text block that was clicked in Figure 16.

Figure 18. If you select multiple text blocks (with the Pointer tool), you'll get a Story Editor window for each story.

Figure 19. Choose Display ¶ from the Story menu while in the Story Editor.

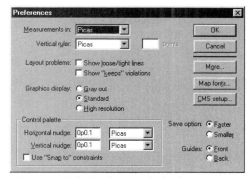

Figure 20. The Preferences dialog box.

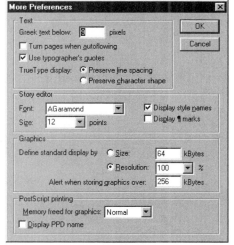

Figure 21. The More Preferences dialog box. The center of this box contains some Story Editor preferences.

To view invisible characters in the Story Editor:

Choose Story⇨Display ¶ (Figure 19).

All the invisible characters, such as spaces, tabs, paragraph returns, and line breaks (see Chapter 10) appear.

To change the font and type size in the Story Editor:

1. **Choose File⇨Preferences.**

   The Preferences dialog box appears (**Figure 20**).

2. **Click the More button.**

   The More Preferences dialog box appears (**Figure 21**).

3. **Change the font and size in the middle section, marked Story editor.**

4. **Click OK.**

   The Preferences dialog box appears again.

5. **Click OK.**

   The font in the Story Editor has changed to your selection.

Story Editor Options

OBJECT MANAGEMENT

16

Organizing your artwork and text in PageMaker can be an all-consuming task. Fortunately, there are many tools and features that make this process much smoother.

The Control palette can be used to precisely position, scale, and rotate objects. You can use PageMaker's grids and guides to keep objects orderly. Finally you can use the built-in alignment and distribution tools to place your objects more consistently.

Introduction to Object Management

The Control palette

So far, we've used two different versions of the Control palette: one for adjusting character attributes, and another for adjusting paragraph attributes. There's a third version, however, and depending on the type of work you do, you'll find yourself using it even more than the character and paragraph versions.

In order to see this "object" view of the Control palette, you must have one or more objects selected with the Pointer tool. The selection type indicator (far left on the palette) will tell you what type of selection it is. **Figure 1** shows each of the different selection type icons and their meanings.

The measurement system used in the Control palette (**Figure 2**) is the same as the one currently set in General Preferences (Ctrl+K).

Display the Control palette by choosing Window⇨Show Control Palette (Ctrl+'). This chapter assumes the Control palette remains open on your screen all the time (which is a really good idea).

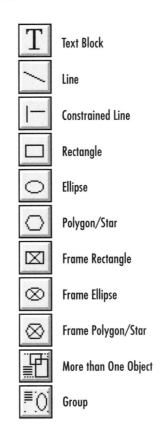

Figure 1. The different symbols that appear depending on what is selected with the Pointer tool.

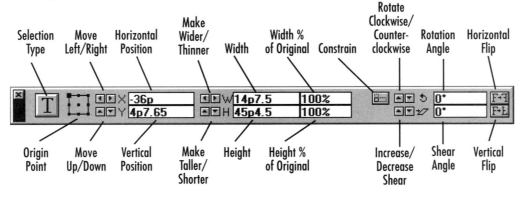

Figure 2. The Control palette when objects are selected with the Pointer tool.

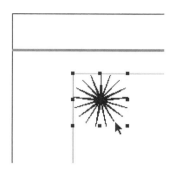

Figure 3. Select the object you wish to move.

Figure 4. Choose the upper-left origin point.

Figure 5. Double-click the X field to highlight it.

Figure 6. Enter the X value and press the Tab key to highlight the Y field.

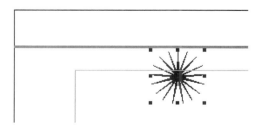

Figure 7. The object is moved to the new location.

To position an object at a specific location:

1. Select the object using the Pointer tool (**Figure 3**).

2. In the Control palette, click the upper-left corner of the Origin Point indicator (**Figure 4**).

   In some cases, you'll want to choose another corner, the center, or an edge, but for these examples we'll be using the upper-left corner.

3. Double-click in the X text field (**Figure 5**).

   The value in the X text field will be highlighted.

4. Type in the distance that the object should be from the left edge of the page, and press the Tab key.

   The Y text field (for vertical position) becomes highlighted (**Figure 6**).

5. Type in the distance that the object should be from the top of the page and press the Return or Enter key.

   The object is moved to the new location (**Figure 7**).

Precise Positioning with the Control Palette

To scale an object to a specific size:

1. Select the object (or objects) you wish to scale (**Figure 8**).

2. In the Control palette, change the W value to the width you wish the object to be (**Figure 9**).

   I typed in picas, but you could type in your width using any measurement system.

3. Press the Tab key.

   The H value is highlighted.

4. Change the H value to the height you wish the object to be (**Figure 10**).

5. Press the Enter key.

   The object is scaled to the size you've entered (**Figure 11**).

To scale an object by percentage:

1. Select the object (or objects) you wish to scale.

2. In the Control palette, change the value (to the right of the W value) to the percent you wish to scale the width of the object and press the Tab key.

3. Change the highlighted value (to the right of the H value) to the percent you wish the object to be.

4. Press the Enter key.

   The object is scaled to the new percentage.

Figure 8. Select the object you wish to scale.

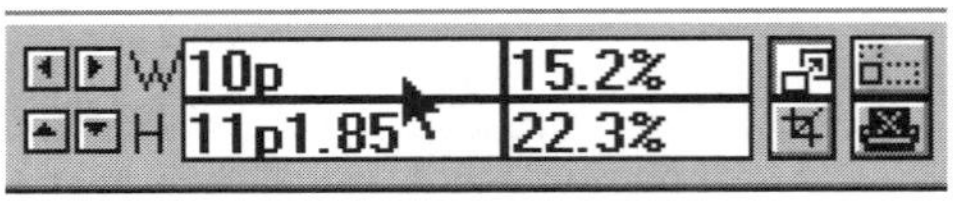

Figure 9. Enter a value in the W field of the Control palette to change the width.

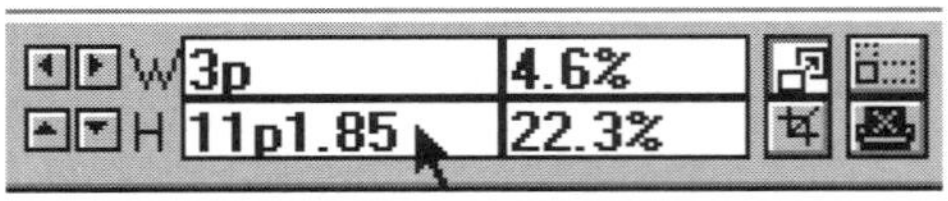

Figure 10. Enter a value in the H field to change the height.

Figure 11. After pressing the Enter key, the object is scaled to your specified dimensions. Even if that means crushing your cat.

Figure 12. Select the object you wish to scale.

Figure 13. Click the Constrain icon so that it looks like this.

Figure 14. The Constrain icon set to non-proportional scaling.

Figure 15. The object after being proportionately scaled to 50%.

To scale an object proportionately:

1. Select the object you wish to scale (**Figure 12**).

2. Click the Constrain icon so it matches the proportional constrain icon shown in **Figure 13**.

   If it already appears this way, clicking it will change it to the non-proportional constrain icon (**Figure 14**).

3. Double-click on any value in the scaling area: W, H, or the two percentage text fields.

   Because you're scaling proportionately, changing any one of these values will change the other ones automatically.

4. Enter a new value and click OK (**Figure 15**).

   The object will be scaled proportionately to the dimension you entered.

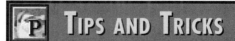

TIPS AND TRICKS

When scaling text blocks, the text inside is *not* scaled, whether you're scaling proportionately or not. To increase or decrease the size of text, you must select it with the Text tool and use the type sizing controls.

Scaling Proportionately

To rotate an object:

1. Select the object you wish to rotate (**Figure 16**).

2. In the Control palette, change the rotation text field to the angle you wish to rotate the object (**Figure 17**).

3. Press the Enter key.

   The object is rotated to the angle you've entered (**Figure 18**).

Figure 16. Select the object you wish to rotate.

![TIPS AND TRICKS]

TIPS AND TRICKS

Entering a positive number in the rotation angle text field will rotate the object counterclockwise. Entering a negative number rotates the image clockwise. It is usually easier on your brain to enter a value of -60° than to type in 300°.

Figure 17. Enter the angle of rotation in the rotation text field within the Control palette.

Figure 18. The object after being rotated 32° (counterclockwise).

Figure 19. Select the object you wish to shear.

Figure 20. Enter the degree of shearing in the shear text field within the Control palette.

Figure 21. The object after being sheared 15˚. Funny, he looks like he could still use a good clipping.

Shearing

Shearing (think of windshear) is the process of sliding one edge of an image in one direction, while the opposite edge remains in the same place. For instance, shearing typically involves sliding the top edge of an image to the left or right, while the bottom of the image remains in place. This gives the image a slanted look.

To shear an object:

1. **Select the object you wish to shear (Figure 19).**

2. **In the Control palette, change the shear text field to the angle you wish to shear the object (Figure 20).**

3. **Press the Enter key.**

   The object is sheared to the angle you've entered (**Figure 21**).

![P] TIPS AND TRICKS

While the origin point is important when performing any of the Control palette transformations, it is critical when shearing. The origin point becomes the anchor which will not move, while the rest of the image is sheared from that point.

Shearing

To flip a text block horizontally:

1. Select the text block you wish to flip (**Figure 22**).

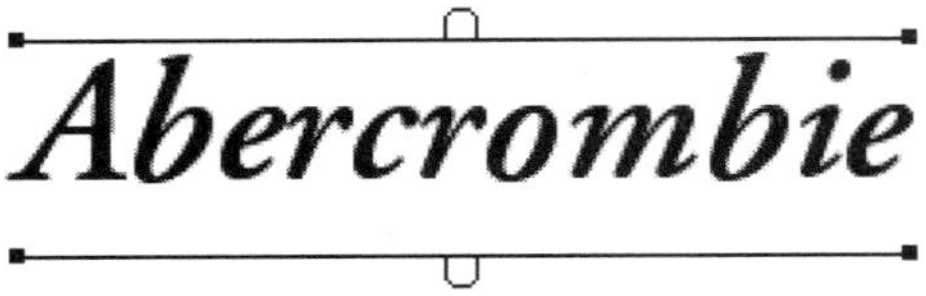

2. Click the Horizontal Flip button on the Control palette (**Figure 23**).

   The entire text block will be flipped horizontally (**Figure 24**).

To flip a text block vertically:

1. Select the text block you wish to flip.

2. Click the Vertical Flip button on the Control palette (right below the Horizontal Flip button).

   The entire text block will be flipped vertically.

To flip a picture horizontally:

1. Select the picture you wish to flip (**Figure 25**).

2. Click the Horizontal Flip button on the Control palette.

   The entire text block will be flipped horizontally (**Figure 26**).

To flip a picture vertically:

1. Select the picture you wish to flip.

2. Click the Vertical Flip button on the Control palette.

   The entire picture will be flipped vertically.

Figure 22. Select the text block to be flipped.

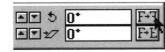

Figure 23. Click the Horizontal Flip button.

Figure 24. The text block after being flipped.

Figure 25. Select the picture you wish to flip.

Figure 26. Flippidy Bippidy.

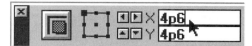

Figure 27. Click to the right of the current X value (don't double-click).

Figure 28. Type + followed by the distance you wish to move the object.

How the Control palette doubles as a calculator

All of the numerical entry text fields in the Control palette can be modified using mathematical operations. For instance, if you wanted to move a text block, currently 1p8.3 from the left edge of the document, exactly 2.15" to the right, you could do it this way:

To move an object using addition in the Control palette:

1. With the Pointer tool, select the object you wish to move.

2. In the Control palette, click to the right of the current X value (Figure 27).

   Instead of highlighting the X value, a blinking cursor appears to the right of it.

3. Type + after the value, and then the amount you wish to move the object (to the right) (Figure 28).

4. Press the Enter key.

   If a positive value is entered, the object will move that distance to the right.

   If you enter a negative value, the object will move that distance to the left.

   You can also enter values in the vertical movement (Y) text field to move objects up (using a negative number) or down (using a positive number).

TIPS AND TRICKS

Besides addition and subtraction operations, you can also do multiplication and division by using the * for multiplication and / for division.

Math and the Control Palette

209

The Grid Manger

The Grid Manager is a dialog box which gives you complete control over columns, gutters, and other guides on your page.

To use the Grid Manager:

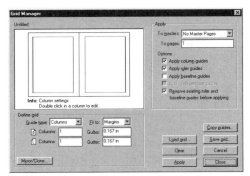

Figure 29. The Grid Manager dialog box.

1. Choose Utilities ⇨ Plug-Ins ⇨ Grid Manager.

   The Grid Manager dialog box appears (**Figure 29**).

2. In the Define grid section, choose the guide type from the Guide type pop-up menu.

   You can choose to define columns, ruler guides, and baseline guides.

3. For each guide type, adjust the attributes for that type.

   For instance, for columns, you would adjust the number of columns on the left and right pages, and the gutter (or empty space) between those columns.

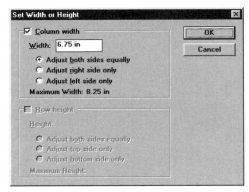

Figure 30. Double-clicking on a column in the preview area displays this dialog box.

4. If you want to adjust an individual column, double-click in that column to edit it.

   The Set Width or Height dialog box will appear, where you can enter specific values to adjust column size (**Figure 30**).

5. Click OK to exit the Set Width or Height dialog box.

   The box will close.

6. Click the Close button to apply the changes and close the Grid Manager dialog box.

Using the Grid Manager

Figure 31. Choose Show Rulers from the View menu.

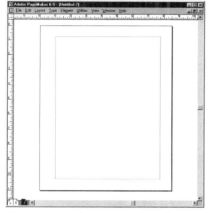

Figure 32. Rulers appear along the top and left edges of your document window.

Figure 33. Dragging a guide from the ruler places that ruler guide in the document.

To create a ruler guide:

1. View rulers by choosing View⇨Show Rulers (Ctrl+R) (Figure 31).

   Rulers will appear along the top and left edges of your document window (**Figure 32**).

2. **Click and drag from the ruler onto the document page.**

   As you drag, a dotted line will accompany your cursor, parallel to the ruler you dragged it from.

3. **Release the mouse button.**

   A ruler guide will appear in your document (**Figure 33**).

To change the origin of your ruler guides:

1. **Click at the point where the two ruler guides meet and drag into your document.**

   Crosshairs will appear under your cursor, with a line extending across the page.

2. **Release the mouse button.**

   The ruler origin has changed. All measurements are now based on the new origin.

To reset the ruler origin:

Double-click on the origin point.

The default location of the rulers changes to zero in the upper-left corner of each document page.

Ruler Guides

Aligning and Distributing Objects

To align objects:

1. Using the Pointer tool, select the objects you wish to align (**Figure 34**).

2. Choose Element ➪ Align Objects (**Ctrl+Shift+E**) (**Figure 35**).

   The Align Objects dialog box appears (**Figure 36**).

3. In the Align Objects dialog box, choose the type of horizontal and vertical alignment you would like to use.

   For my example, I chose the "Align Tops" option (**Figure 36**).

4. Click the OK button.

   The objects are aligned along their top edges (**Figure 37**).

Distributing objects

I used the Distribute options to evenly space the figures and captions on each page throughout this book. I grouped the captions to the images, positioned the top and bottom figures at the top and bottom of the column, then chose the vertical Distribute Edges option (upper-right button) in the Align Objects dialog box.

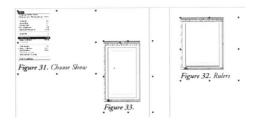

Figure 31. Choose Show   *Figure 32. Rulers*

Figure 33.

Figure 34. Select the objects you wish to align.

Figure 35. Choose Align Objects from the Element Menu.

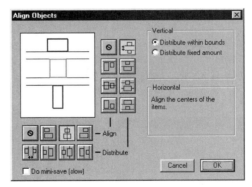

Figure 36. The Align Objects dialog box.

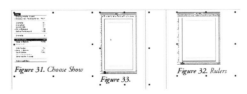

Figure 31. Choose Show   *Figure 32. Rulers*

Figure 33.

Figure 37. The objects after being aligned along their top edges.

TIPS AND TRICKS

In order to align objects, you must have at least two selected. In order to use the distribution capabilities of Align Objects, you must have at least three objects selected.

The more complex your documents are, the more you'll appreciate PageMaker's layers capabilities. Layers allow you to link certain objects together without actually grouping them, which makes selecting objects and manipulating them easier than ever.

While creating this book in PageMaker, I used layers in the most basic of ways: to keep figures and the accompanying text separate. I also kept the tips and thumb tab text (the text that appears sideways on the edge of each page) on their own layers.

Introduction to Layers

The Layers palette

The Layers palette is the nerve center for organizing your artwork with layers.

To view the Layers palette:

Choose Window⇨Show Layers (Ctrl+8) (Figure 1).

The Layers palette will appear (Figure 2).

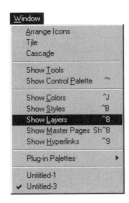

Figure 1. Choose Show Layers from the Window menu.

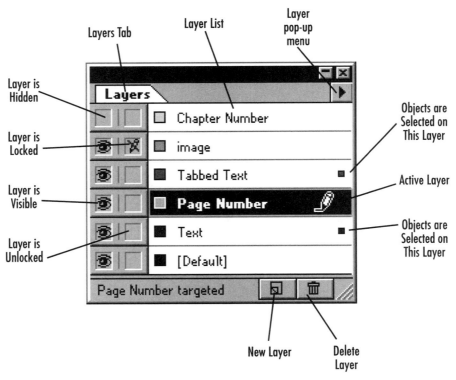

Figure 2. The Layers palette.

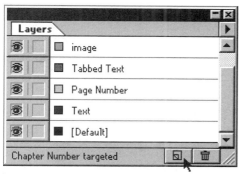

Figure 3. Click the New Layer icon in the Layers palette to create a new layer.

Figure 4. The New Layer dialog box.

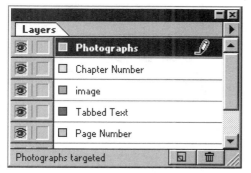

Figure 5. The new layer appears at the top of the Layers palette.

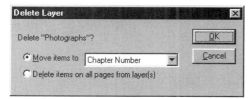

Figure 6. The warning dialog box that appears when you try to delete a layer containing objects.

To create a new layer:

1. **Click the New Layer icon in the Layers palette (Figure 3).**

   The New Layer dialog box appears (**Figure 4**).

2. **Type in a name for the layer.**

   Use a descriptive name that accurately defines what will be on that layer. Avoid just hitting the Enter key and letting PageMaker name the layer "Layer 2" for you.

3. **Pick a color for the layer.**

   PageMaker assigns a different color to each layer that is created. However, sometimes I like to use similar colors for layers that are similar. For instance, I would choose aqua for my page number layer, and choose blue for my running heads layer.

4. **Click the OK button.**

   The layer will be added to the top of the layer list in the Layers palette (**Figure 5**).

To remove a layer:

1. **Select the layer you wish to remove.**

2. **Either click the trash can icon or drag the layer to the trash can.**

   If items exist on the layer you're removing, a dialog box will ask where (which layer) to move those objects (**Figure 6**).

To place an object on a layer:

1. **Select the object you want to move to a layer (Figure 7).**

   When any object is selected in PageMaker, a little square appears in the Layers palette next to the layer that contains the selected object (**Figure 8**).

2. **In the Layers palette, click and drag the colored square to the target layer, then release the mouse button.**

   The object is moved to the new layer, and the little square now appears on that layer in the Layers palette (**Figure 9**).

To create an object on a specific layer:

1. **Click on the layer in which you want to create an object.**

   The layer you click on will become highlighted and display a little pencil (**Figure 10**). This indicates that this layer is the *active* layer, and all new objects will be created on this layer.

2. **Create your object.**

   If you create the object with a tool other than the Text tool, you'll see a little square to the right of the layer name, indicating that there is an object selected on that layer. The Text tool allows you to keep on typing, without actually selecting the text block.

Figure 7. Select the object you wish to move.

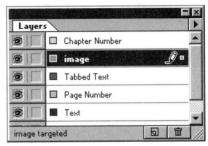

Figure 8. A colored square appears to the right of the layer name.

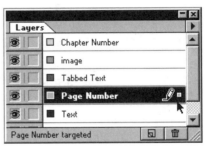

Figure 9. Drag the colored square to a different layer; the object will be moved to that layer.

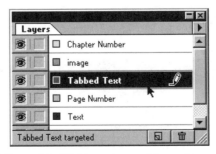

Figure 10. Clicking a layer with no objects selected makes that layer the active layer.

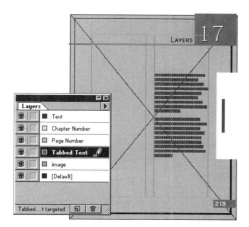

Figure 11. Layers the way they're supposed to be for this chapter.

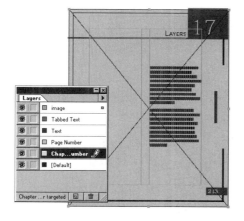

Figure 12. After some creative manipulation of layer orders, some of the items look different.

Layer shuffling

Not only are layers good for organizing artwork, but they're also good for making sure certain objects stay in front of (or behind) other objects. The layers at the top of the list are placed on top of the layers below them.

Moving a layer up and down through the layer list allows you to quickly place all text in front of all images (if you have text on one layer and images on another), or vice versa. I use layers in this way to make sure that text is in front of screens, and that background images are indeed behind text and other images.

Figure 11 shows the Layers palette and the first page of this chapter as it should be. **Figure 12** shows what it looks like after I've shuffled the layers around a bit. Keep in mind that layers work on an entire document, so adjusting layer positions for specific pages might not be a good idea (it's usually wiser to create special layers for pages with special requirements, so that the rest of the document is unaffected).

To move a layer through the Layers list:

Click and drag the layer you wish to move up or down through the list. When it is in the location you wish it to be, release the mouse button.

The layer will move to that location in the layer list.

Moving Layers in the Layers List

While most of PageMaker deals with composing pages, this chapter in particular focuses on working with the pages themselves. In it, you'll learn how to insert new pages into a document, remove existing pages, move between pages, and sort pages in a large document.

To go to a specific page in a document:

Click on the page number icon along the bottom left of your document window that you wish to go to (**Figure 1**).

You will automatically be taken to that page.

There's another, slightly more complex, way to change pages, which can be useful in a big document where you can't see all the page icons for the document:

1. Choose Layout ⇨ Go to Page (**Ctrl+Alt+G**) (**Figure 2**).

   The Go to Page dialog box appears (**Figure 3**).

2. Type in the page number you wish to go to and click OK.

   That page will be displayed.

Often, I'll just want to turn the page to the next page or to the previous page. This is done by pressing the Page Down (for the next page) or the Page Up (for the previous page) key on my keyboard. This is much faster, even when I want to move forward or backward through my document by a couple of pages.

The Page Up and Page Down keys actually don't move a page at a time, they move a *spread* at a time. This is important because in a typical left/right spread document (this book contains just that), you'll be moving two pages at a time each time you press one of those keys.

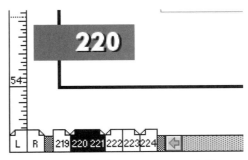

Figure 1. Click the page icon to quickly go to that page.

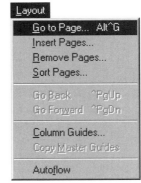

Figure 2. Choose Go to Page from the Layout menu.

Figure 3. The Go to Page dialog box.

Figure 4. Choose Insert Pages from the Layout menu.

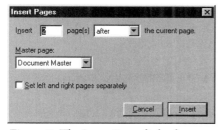

Figure 5. The Insert Pages dialog box.

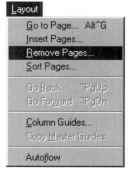

Figure 6. Choose Remove Pages from the Layout menu to remove certain pages from your document.

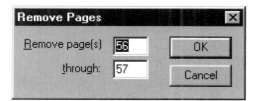

Figure 7. The Remove Pages dialog box.

To insert one or more pages:

1. **Go to the page immediately before the pages you want to insert.**

   You can also go to the page after the pages you want to insert (via an option in the Insert Pages dialog box), but typically you'll want to add pages after existing pages.

2. **Choose Layout ⇨Insert Pages (Figure 4).**

   The Insert Pages dialog box appears (**Figure 5**).

3. **Enter the number of pages you want to insert after the current page.**

   If you want to insert pages before the current page, change the pop-up to the right of the Insert page field to "before." If you're working in a document with left/right page spreads, you can also choose "between," which puts the new pages between the current pages of the spread.

4. **Click the OK button.**

   The new pages are inserted in your document.

To remove one or more pages:

1. **Choose Layout ⇨Remove Pages (Figure 6).**

   The Remove Pages dialog box appears (**Figure 7**).

2. **Enter the page range you wish to remove and click OK.**

Inserting and Removing Pages

221

Sorting pages

PageMaker contains a very handy method for organizing pages in a document. This allows you to quickly move page 3 between pages 4 and 5. If you're working with spreads, you can move pages 8 and 9 between the 4 and 5 spread and the 6 and 7 spread. This is all done with the Sort Pages dialog box.

Figure 8. Choose Sort Pages from the Layout menu.

To move pages within your document:

1. **Choose Layout ⇨ Sort Pages (Figure 8).**

   The Sort Pages dialog box appears, showing all the pages in the current document (**Figure 9**). You may have to make the dialog box larger (by dragging the lower-right corner down and to the right) to see all of your pages.

2. **Click on the page (or spread) that you want to move, and drag it between two other pages or spreads.**

   The page will move between those pages, as indicated by the original page numbers below or next to the pages surrounded by a dotted page edge (**Figure 10**).

   You can select more than one page (or spread) at a time by Shift-clicking on additional pages.

3. **Click the OK button.**

   The pages are rearranged in your document. You may want to look through your document pages to make sure everything is in order.

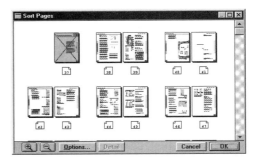

Figure 9. The Sort Pages dialog box.

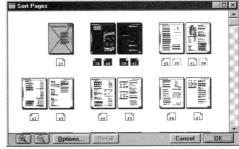

Figure 10. After the second spread has been moved before the first spread.

Figure 11. Choose Document Setup from the File menu.

Figure 12. The Document Setup dialog box.

Figure 13. I created this text by pressing Ctrl+Alt+P, which displays the current page number.

To change the starting page number in a document:

1. **Choose File ⇨ Document Setup (Ctrl+Shift+P) (Figure 11).**

   The Document Setup dialog box appears (**Figure 12**).

2. **Enter a different Start page number.**

   If you're working on a document that includes spreads, make sure your first page is an odd number— if the first page of the document is a right page, or even if the first page is a left page. Remember, most people expect to see even numbers on the left, and odd numbers on the right of printed documents.

3. **Click OK.**

   The document's page numbers change to reflect the new start page.

To place a page number on a page:

1. **Using the Text tool, click where you want the page number to be.**

2. **Press Ctrl+Alt+P, and the current page number will appear (Figure 13).**

   If you change the Start page number, or sort your pages, the page number will be adjusted to reflect the correct number.

Page Numbers

Master pages contain objects that should appear on each page within your document. These objects can't be modified on the document pages, so they can't be accidentally changed.

Master pages can automate a number of the more tedious page layout tasks. Chores like placing page numbers or chapter headings on each page can be done once for the entire document. And, you can change all the pages in the document by just changing what is on the master page.

PageMaker even allows you to have multiple master pages, so that you can have several different consistent styles within a single document.

The Master Pages palette

This palette allows you to create, edit, and apply master pages to document pages. Technically, you never *have* to use the Master Pages palette. It will make using master pages more convenient only when you're working with more than one set of master pages. Otherwise, you might never need it at all.

Figure 1. Choose Show Master Pages from the Window menu to display the Master Pages palette.

To display the Master Pages palette:

Choose Window⇨Show Master Pages (Ctrl+Alt+8) (Figure 1).

The Master Pages palette appears (**Figure 2**).

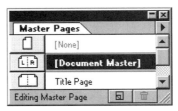

Figure 2. The Master Pages palette.

To create a new master page:

1. **Click the New Master Page button in the Master Pages palette (the little piece of paper to the left of the trash can button).**

   The New Master Page dialog box appears (**Figure 3**).

Figure 3. After clicking the New Master Page icon, the New Master Page dialog box appears.

2. **Enter the name of this master page and click the OK button.**

   A new master page appears in the Master Pages palette (**Figure 4**). In addition, you'll be taken to the master page display (just as if you had clicked on the leftmost pages at the bottom left of your document window). This can be a bit shocking, as it appears that your entire page has vanished...it's still there, you're just viewing the new master page.

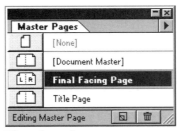

Figure 4. The palette after a new master page has been added to it.

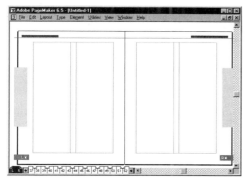

Figure 5. The master pages used for most of the spreads in this book.

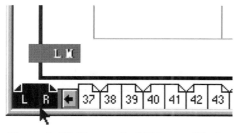

Figure 6. Clicking on the L/R icons will take you to the master page for the page you're currently on. Once you're there, you can change master pages in the Master Pages palette.

Master pages

PageMaker uses master pages to create an uneditable background for each document page. When you put an element on a master page, it will appear on each page in your document, or, if you choose, specific pages to which you assign that master page.

When producing this book, I created different master pages for the chapter opening page and for most spreads. The spread master page (shown in **Figure 5**), contains all the shaded boxes, along with the folios (page numbers and chapter title) that appear on each page. Because those elements don't change, I can use them when creating pages.

To add an item to a master page:

1. **Click on the master page icons (the pages with an L or R in them) at the bottom left of the document window (Figure 6).**

    The document window will display the master pages for that document. If this is a new document, the master pages will be blank.

2. **Using any of PageMaker's tools, add text, an object, or place an image.**

    You can place any object on a master page that PageMaker normally uses.

3. **Return to the document by clicking any page icon along the bottom left of the document window.**

How Master Pages Work

To duplicate a master page:

1. In the Master Pages palette, drag the master page you want to duplicate to the New Master Page icon (**Figure 7**).

   The Duplicate Master Page dialog box appears (**Figure 8**).

2. Name the new master page.

   You might want to keep the default name with the word "copy" after it, so you know it was based on that original master page.

3. Click the Duplicate button.

   The duplicate of the master page will appear in the palette (**Figure 9**).

To delete a master page:

1. In the Master Pages palette, choose the master page you want to delete and drag it to the trash can icon in the palette.

   A warning dialog box appears, asking if you're sure you want to delete that master page (**Figure 10**).

2. Click the OK button.

   The master page will be deleted.

   Any document pages that used that master page will have all master page items removed from those pages, but will otherwise remain the same.

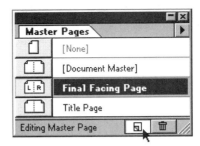

Figure 7. Drag the master page down to the New Master Page icon.

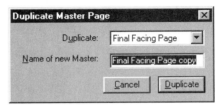

Figure 8. The Duplicate Master Page dialog box.

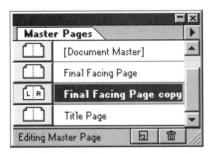

Figure 9. After the duplicate master page has been added to the document, it appears in the Master Pages palette.

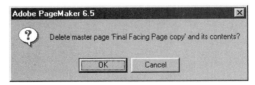

Figure 10. The warning dialog box that appears when you attempt to delete a master page.

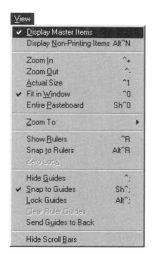

Figure 11. Choose Display Master Items from the View menu. Remove the checkmark to hide all master page items.

To turn off master page items on a document page:

Choose View⇨Display Master Items (Figure 11).

When you release the mouse button, the master page items on that document page are hidden.

Figure 12 shows this spread without Master Page items displayed. This should give you a good idea of what was used on the master page for this spread.

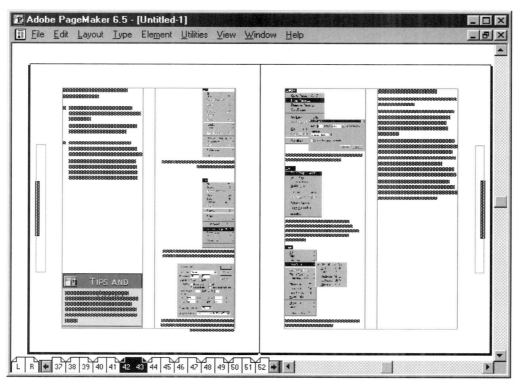

Figure 12. This spread without Master Page items showing.

PART

V

FINISHING

BOOK FUNCTIONS

PageMaker has extraordinary long document capabilities. PageMaker documents can be linked together to form a book, which automatically updates page numbers when pages in individual documents are added or removed. It also keeps track of items in a table of contents and can automatically index words for you.

Books

While PageMaker can theoretically create documents that are hundreds, or even thousands of pages long, it isn't practical to do so. First of all, opening, saving, and navigating through a giant document can grind PageMaker to a halt on the fastest system (you actually go backward in time momentarily on slower systems). Second, PageMaker documents become unstable when they're too large. An unstable document can result in a corrupted file that you may be unable to open—which, as you might guess, is a very bad thing.

Usually, it's a good idea to split potentially long documents into several smaller parts. I created a separate PageMaker document for each chapter in this book. Fortunately, PageMaker has a Book function which helps automate this task.

To combine several documents into a book:

1. **Choose Utilities ⇨ Book (Figure 1).**
   The Book Publication List dialog box appears (**Figure 2**).

2. **Locate each portion of the document you want to add to the book, and click the Insert button.**
   This adds the document to the list on the right side of the dialog box. **Figure 3** shows a book publication list with several chapters from this book added to it.

3. **Click OK.**

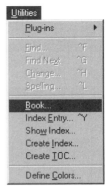

Figure 1. Choose Book from the Utilities menu.

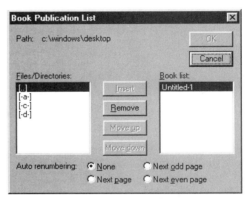

Figure 2. The Book Publication List dialog box.

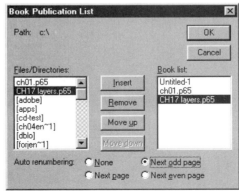

Figure 3. The dialog box after several chapters have been added, and the Next odd page option has been checked, which forces each new document to be numbered as an odd page.

Combining Documents into Books

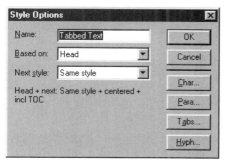

Figure 4. Double-click the style in the Styles palette to view the Style Options dialog box.

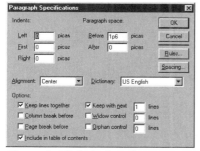

Figure 5. Click the Para button to view the Paragraph Specifications dialog box, then click the Include in table of contents checkbox.

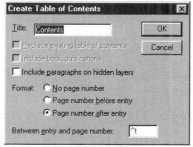

Figure 6. The Create Table of Contents dialog box.

Contents

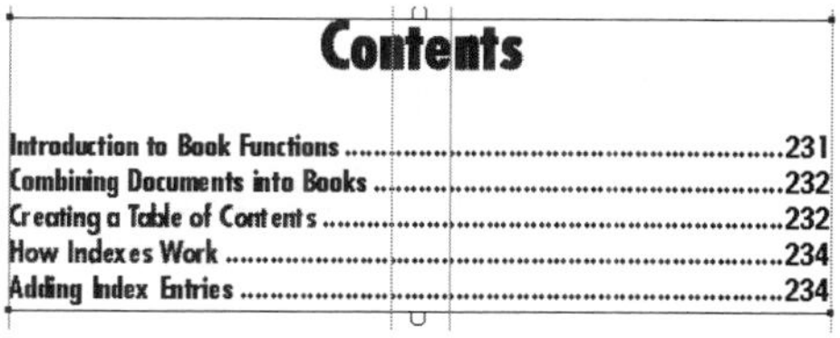

Figure 7. The Contents text that was generated for this chapter.

To create a table of contents:

1. **In the Styles palette, double-click on the style you want to use for your table of contents listings.**

   The Style Options dialog box for that style appears (**Figure 4**).

   You don't *have* to use a style for table of contents (TOC) entries, but if you don't, you'll have to manually select each paragraph to be used in the TOC, choose Paragraph from the Type menu, and go to step 3.

2. **Click the Para button.**

   The Paragraph Specifications dialog box appears (**Figure 5**).

3. **Click the Include in table of contents checkbox, and click OK to exit the Paragraph Specifications dialog box, and click OK to exit the Style Options dialog box.**

4. **Choose Utilities ⇨ Create TOC.**

   The Create Table of Contents dialog box appears (**Figure 6**).

5. **Click OK.**

   Your cursor will change into the text placement cursor.

6. **Click with the cursor in the column where you want to place your TOC.**

   A table of contents appears, using the style you selected in the previous steps (**Figure 7**). In this book, I used the style Tabbed Text for my Table of Contents entries (so that the text along the outside edge of the page would match the TOC headings).

Indexes

PageMaker has an excellent integrated index creation system, although it does take a bit of work to initially set up the index. Using it, you can automatically create index entries for an entire publication in minutes (providing you took the time to set it all up correctly).

PageMaker's indexes allow you to define what words go into the index and how those words should appear. For instance, if I wanted the word Floober to appear in my index, I could set it up as an entry, or more appropriately set it up as a sub-entry of Plysen Dots (a Floober, as everyone knows, is one of a dozen different Plysen Dots).

The following page describes how to add entries to an index.

To create an index:

1. **Choose Utilities ⇨ Create Index (Figure 8).**
   The Create Index dialog box appears (**Figure 9**).

2. **Click the Format button.**
   The Index Format dialog box appears (**Figure 10**).

3. **Make any changes to the format of the index and click OK.**

4. **Click OK again.**
   The cursor changes to the text placeholder.

5. **Click in the column where you want your index to begin.**

Figure 8. Choose Create Index from the Utilities menu.

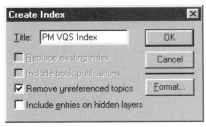

Figure 9. The Create Index dialog box.

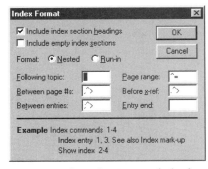

Figure 10. The Index Format dialog box, accessed by clicking the Format button in the Create Index dialog box.

TIPS AND TRICKS

For a listing of all of those scary-looking codes in the Index Format dialog box, see your PageMaker User Guide.

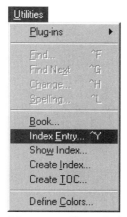

Figure 11. Select the word or phrase you want to add as an index entry.

Figure 12. Choose Index Entry from the Utilities menu.

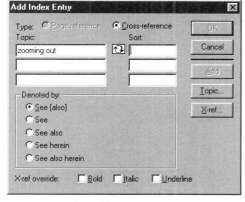

Figure 13. The Add Index Entry dialog box.

To add an entry to an index:

1. **Select the word (or words) you want as an index entry (Figure 11).**

   You don't have to select a specific entry, but doing so ensures that spelling is correct and that the word you're entering does indeed exist in your document. If you don't select a word, you'll have to enter the word in the Index Entry dialog box by typing it in.

2. **Choose Utilities ⇨Index Entry (Ctrl+Y) (Figure 12).**

   The Add Index Entry dialog box appears with the first entry word or words you highlighted (**Figure 13**).

3. **Click OK.**

   That entry is now added to your index.

Adding Index Entries

One of PageMaker's extremely useful functions involves repurposing your PageMaker documents as World Wide Web pages. PageMaker 6.5 was especially designed with this in mind, to take advantage of HTML and Web capabilities. PageMaker has a special menu entry just for creating HTML files from PageMaker documents.

Introduction to Web Pages

HTML is ugly

Compared to the myriad of options PageMaker provides for formatting text, placing images, and laying out pages, HTML documents are awful. Although HTML is still evolving, it will be quite some time before you see HTML web pages that look as refined as PageMaker pages.

However, PageMaker contains an export filter that takes your PageMaker page and transforms it into HTML, almost magically.

HTML can be beautiful

There are a few programs that can turn your HTML pages into lovely things, and can also help you create good-looking pages in the first place. **Figures 1** and **2** show two web pages that were created using a combination of the following products:

Adobe PageMill is the most popular web page creation utility for Macintosh owners, and its interface is similar to PageMaker's.

Claris Home Page is full of good features and is a solid alternative to PageMill.

Microsoft FrontPage is the web page design software from your friends in Seattle.

If you're truly daring, you might want to create a web page using straight HTML code. Yes, its ugly, but you'll have complete control over the way your page works.

Figure 1. The Bezier Inc. Home Page at www.bezier.com.

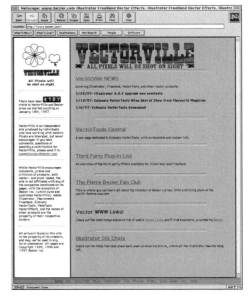

Figure 2. The VectorVille home page at www.bezier.com/vectorville.

Figure 3. Choose HTML from the Export submenu in the File menu.

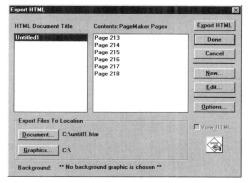

Figure 4. The Export HTML dialog box.

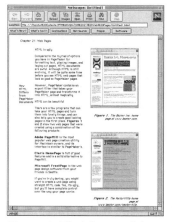

Figure 5. The left page of this spread as it appears in HTML.

To create an HTML web page from a PageMaker document:

1. **Open the PageMaker document.**
   I'm using the document for this chapter as an example.

2. **Choose File ⇨ Export ⇨ HTML (Figure 3).**
   The Export HTML dialog box appears (**Figure 4**).

3. **Make any changes in the box.**
   You can just wing it and click OK, then come back here in the future to modify options based on the appearance of the initial web page.

4. **Click the Export HTML button.**
   PageMaker will display a series of messages telling you about possible problems with your document as it is converted to HTML. In my case, PageMaker displayed several messages regarding the shaded boxes I used behind the page numbers and tab text; I just clicked the OK button for each.

5. **Click the Done button.**
   You'll be returned to your PageMaker document.

To view your new web page:

Drag the document generated by PageMaker (typically called Untitled1) on top of your web browser.

Your newly converted web page will appear (**Figure 5**).

Creating HTML from a PageMaker Document

To add a link to a PageMaker object:

1. Select the object or text you would like to use as a link (**Figure 6**).

   If you want text within a text block to be selected, be sure to use the Text tool.

2. Choose Window⇨Show Hyperlinks (**Ctrl+9**) (**Figure 7**) to display the Hyperlinks palette.

3. Choose New URL from the pop-up menu on the Hyperlinks palette (**Figure 8**).

   The New URL dialog box appears.

4. Enter the URL in the dialog box and click OK.

   The URL appears in the Hyperlinks palette.

5. Click the icon to the left of the URL (**Figure 9**).

   The Source dialog box appears.

6. You can enter the text you have selected, the name of the selected object, or leave the name as Source1, then click OK.

To view your links in PageMaker:

Click on the Hand tool in the toolbox.

All links in your document will be surrounded by a blue frame (**Figure 10**).

My favorite site is Bezier Inc.

Figure 6. Select the text (or object) you want to use as a link.

Figure 7. Choose Show Hyperlinks from the Window menu.

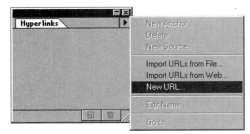

Figure 8. Choose New URL from the Hyperlinks palette pop-up menu.

Figure 9. Click the icon to the left of the URL in the Hyperlinks palette.

My favorite site is Bezier Inc.

Figure 10. When the Hand tool is active, all links appear with a blue frame around them.

CREATING PDF FILES

I'm not sure who is luckier: PageMaker users who benefit from having Acrobat work so seamlessly with PageMaker, or Acrobat users who can use PageMaker as an authoring tool for PDF documents. It's a match made in desktop publishing heaven (where the dpi is infinite, and everything is 100% compatible).

PDF (Portable Document Format) files are cross-platform document standards. Anyone with a copy of the free Acrobat Reader for Mac, Windows, or even UNIX can view an Acrobat PDF Document. PDFs look exactly like the original document, from fonts to photos. It's the perfect format for giving your PageMaker files to people who don't have PageMaker. PageMaker includes Acrobat Distiller, which is the software that transforms your PageMaker documents into PDFs.

Introduction to Creating PDF Files

Portable Document Files

The Acrobat PDF file type is the widely accepted standard for electronic document exchange. There are two reasons for this. First, any program that can print a file can create a PDF file. Second, there's free software for every computer platform/operating system out there, in the form of Acrobat Reader (which ships with each Macintosh, as well as with PageMaker).

In order for you to view a PDF file, you must have Acrobat Reader loaded on your system.

Acrobat Reader 3.0 is software that allows you to read PDF files, a universal cross-platform file type that PageMaker in particular excels at creating.

To install Acrobat Reader:

1. **Insert the PageMaker CD-ROM in your CD-ROM drive.**

   The PM 6.5 Autoplay window will appear (**Figure 1**).

2. **Click once on "Install Acrobat Reader 3.0."**

   This will launch the installation software.

3. **Proceed through the Installation instructions.**

   After installation, you can access Acrobat Reader by double-clicking the AcroRd32 icon in the Reader window (**Figure 2**).

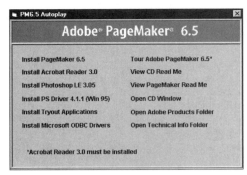

Figure 1. The PM 6.5 Autoplay screen that appears when you insert the PageMaker CD-ROM into your computer.

Figure 2. The Acrobat Reader Window.

TIPS AND TRICKS

If you have purchased Acrobat 3.0, you have a program called Acrobat Exchange, which allows you to both view and edit PDF files (whether they were created with PageMaker or not). You don't need to install Acrobat Reader if Acrobat Exchange is already installed on your system.

How PDF Works

Figure 3. Choose Adobe PDF from the Export submenu of the File menu.

Figure 4. The Export Adobe PDF dialog box.

Figure 5. The Save As dialog box, where you name the PDF file you're creating.

Figure 6. This chapter as it appears in Acrobat.

To create a PDF from a PageMaker document:

1. Open the PageMaker document from which you wish to create a PDF.

2. Choose File ⇨ Export ⇨ Adobe PDF (**Figure 3**).

   The Export Adobe PDF dialog box appears (**Figure 4**).

3. Change any options in the Export Adobe PDF dialog box that need to be adjusted.

   I recommend checking the Distill now radio button and View PDF using checkbox, so that the PDF file is both created and opened for viewing in Acrobat.

4. Click the Export button.

   A dialog box appears, giving you the opportunity to name your PDF file and choose a location where it should be saved (**Figure 5**).

5. Click the Save button.

   All sorts of things will happen on your screen. First, PageMaker will translate the file into PostScript. Next, Acrobat Distiller will be launched automatically, and will process the PostScript files. Finally, the new PDF will open in Acrobat (**Figure 6**). Fortunately, you don't have to do anything after you click the Save button—PageMaker does it all automatically!

Creating a PDF from a PageMaker Document

How fitting that this chapter is the last in the *PageMaker 6.5 for Windows: Visual QuickStart Guide*, as it happens that printing is typically the last thing you do with a PageMaker document. The Last but not Least rule is in effect, of course, because printing is one of the most critical operations surrounding any PageMaker document.

PageMaker's printing features provide a method to control exactly how your document appears on the printed page, from specifying pages to be printed to adjusting which color plates should print.

Introduction to Printing

To prepare a document for printing:

1. **Make sure all the images in the document are current.**

   You can do this quite easily by choosing File⇨Links Manager (Ctrl+Shift+D) (**Figure 1**) and looking for any items with question marks next to them in the Links Manager dialog box (**Figure 2**).

   If you do find items with question marks next to them, click on each item to determine the problem. Usually, clicking either the Link or Update buttons will correct the discrepancy. The Link button will allow you to relink the image in your document to the original image file. Clicking the Update button makes the image placed in your document match the image file.

2. **Make sure your printer is attached to your system and is turned on.**

   If you're using a network printer, be sure that it is connected to the network.

3. **Save your document by choosing File⇨Save (Ctrl+S) (Figure 3).**

   Critical errors seem to occur while printing, so be sure to save your document *before* you attempt to print.

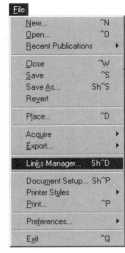

Figure 1. Choose Links Manager from the File menu.

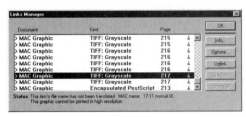

Figure 2. The Links Manager dialog box.

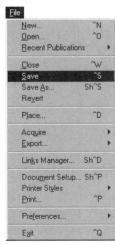

Figure 3. Always Save before you print.

Figure 4. Choose Print from the File menu.

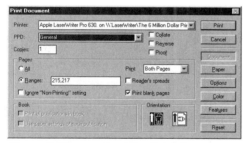

Figure 5. The awe-inspiring Print Document dialog box.

TIPS AND TRICKS

To quickly print a document, I press Ctrl+P and then whack the good ole Enter key (which pushes the Print button in the Print Document dialog box). This takes about a half second, and unless I need to specify which pages should print (see the following page), it's the easiest way to send documents to the printer.

To print your document from PageMaker:

1. **Open the document you wish to print.**

   You can also print a document by selecting its icon in the Finder, and choosing the Print option from the File menu, but then you won't have quite as many options.

2. **Choose File ⇨ Print (Ctrl+P) (Figure 4).**

   The Print Document dialog box appears (**Figure 5**). Although this dialog box seems quite intimidating, you can usually ignore almost everything with the exception of a few controls when printing your documents.

3. **Make sure the All option is chosen in the Pages section.**

   If it isn't, it's possible that not all of the pages in your document will print.

4. **Click the Print button.**

   A few dialog boxes will appear, letting you know that the printing process is taking place. In a small, basic document these can flash by in a few seconds. In a larger document, it could take several minutes until the dialog boxes leave your screen.

   The pages should start churning out of your printer after just a few moments, unless your pages are complex or contain a lot of placed artwork.

Printing a Document

Entering page ranges

PageMaker deals with page ranges a little differently than most other Windows software. Instead of From and To text fields to determine the starting and ending page to be printed, PageMaker allows you to print non-contiguous chunks of pages by entering values in one text field (Ranges). How you enter the numbers in the Ranges text field determines which pages print.

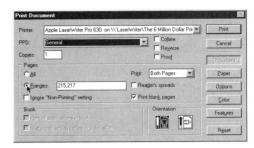

Figure 6. *The Print Document dialog box with the Ranges option checked. This setting would cause two non-contiguous pages to be printed.*

To print a specific range of pages:

1. In the Print Document dialog box, click the Ranges radio button (Figure 6).

2. Enter the page range you would like to print (see below).

3. Click the Print button.

   Only the pages you specified will be printed.

To print contiguous pages:

Enter a page range with a hyphen between the first and last pages.

For instance, to print from page 4 to 8, you would enter the following: 4-8

To print non-contiguous pages:

Enter each page or page range separated by a comma.

For instance, to print pages 6, 8, and 11 through 14, you would enter: 6, 8, 11-14

TIPS AND TRICKS

If you started your document on a page other than page 1, be sure to use the new page numbers when specifying which pages to print. For instance, to print the spread of pages you're looking at, I would *not* specify pages 4-5, even though these are the fourth and fifth pages in the document. Instead, I would enter 250-251, which are the current page numbers.

TIPS AND TRICKS

You can always print a single page by simply entering that page number in the Ranges text field.

Printing to files

In some cases, you'll want to print your document directly to your hard drive in the form of a PostScript file. This file can be sent to any PostScript printer, or distilled by Acrobat Distiller into a PDF document.

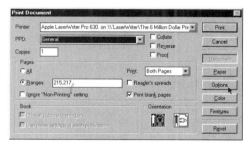

Figure 7. The Print Document dialog box. Click the Options button to be able to print to a PostScript file.

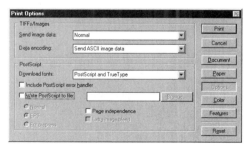

Figure 8. The Print Options dialog box.

To print to a file (instead of to a printer):

1. **Choose File ⇨ Print.**

   The Print Document dialog box appears (**Figure 7**).

2. **Click the Options button in the Print Document dialog box.**

   The Print Options dialog box appears (**Figure 8**).

3. **Click the Write PostScript to file checkbox.**

   Checking this box allows you to enter a name for the file.

4. **To the right of the box you just checked, enter the name of the PostScript file you'd like to create.**

   By clicking the Save as button, you can define the location as well as the name of the file. If you don't specify a location, the PostScript file will be saved in the same folder as your PageMaker document.

5. **Click the Print button.**

   The PostScript file will be written to your hard drive.

   The PostScript file you've created can be downloaded to any printer using a utility such as LaserWriter Utility. These files can be extremely large, so keep several megabytes of free space on the destination disk.

Printing to a File

To print color separations:

1. In the Print Document dialog box, click the Color button (Figure 9).

   The Print Color dialog box appears (Figure 10).

2. Choose the Separations option.

3. Click the Print button.

   Separations for each color in your document will be printed.

How separations work

If you only have black in your document, the only page that will be printed will be a black separation. If you have full color artwork or photographs, you'll get a separate sheet for cyan, magenta, yellow, and black. If you have objects in the document that contain spot colors, a sheet for each spot color will be printed.

To print a specific color:

1. In the Print Document dialog box, click the Color button.

2. Choose the Separations option in the Print Color dialog box.

3. In the list of separations, scroll to the color you wish to print, and double-click on it (Figure 11).

   A checkmark will appear next to that color. Double-clicking on a color that has a checkmark will remove the checkmark and prevent that color from printing.

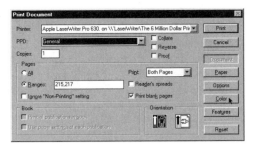

Figure 9. Click the Color button in the Print Document dialog box.

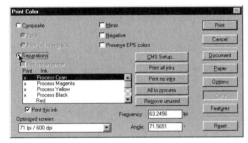

Figure 10. Choose the Separations option in the Print Color dialog box.

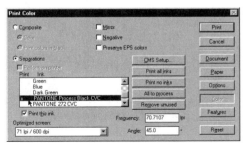

Figure 11. Scroll to the color you wish to print, and double-click on that color. When a checkmark appears next to a color, that color will print.

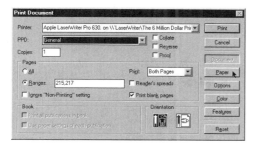

Figure 12. Click the Paper button in the Print Document dialog box.

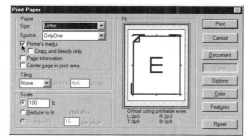

Figure 13. Click the Printer's marks checkbox in the Print Paper dialog box.

Crop marks

Printing crop marks can be useful if your printed page needs to be trimmed (if you'll be printing on paper that is larger than the document size). Crop marks appear automatically on printouts of both composite and separation printouts.

To print a document with crop marks:

1. **In the Print Document dialog box, click the Paper button (Figure 12).**

   The Print Paper dialog box appears (**Figure 13**).

2. **Click the Printer's marks checkbox.**

   Checking the inset box, "Crops and bleeds only" prevents additional information, such as registration marks and color bars from appearing on your page. Only check that box if you'll be printing single color documents.

3. **Click the Print button.**

   The image will be printed with crop marks.

Printing Crop Marks

Printer Styles

If you find yourself constantly going between two or more different sets of printing options, you'll find PageMaker's "hidden" feature of Printer Styles a godsend. For instance, I'm constantly printing out documents to my black and white laser printer that need cropmarks, to my color printer without bleeds or cropmarks but sized smaller to fit on the color sheets, and to PostScript files, where I have other special requirements.

PageMaker lets me set up each of these combinations of printing options as Printer Styles. When I want to print, I can choose the proper printer style from the File menu, and then press Enter.

To use an existing Printer Style:

1. **Choose File ➪ Printer Styles ➪ YourStyle (Figure 14).**

    Note that YourStyle is the printer style you wish to use. The Print Document dialog box appears with the settings for that Printer Style already in place (**Figure 15**).

2. **In the Print Document dialog box, click the Print button.**

    The document will be printed with the printer options that are defined for that Printer Style.

Figure 14. Choose a predefined printer style from the Printer Styles submenu in the File menu.

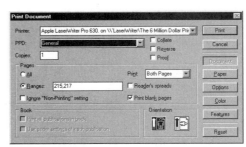

Figure 15. The Print Document dialog box appears with all the settings defined in that Printer Style already in place.

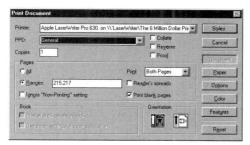

Figure 16. The Print button changes into the Styles button when you press the Ctrl key.

Figure 17. The Rename Printer Style dialog box.

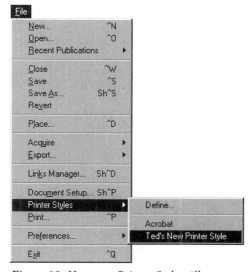

Figure 18. Your new Printer Style will appear in the Printer Styles submenu of the File menu.

To create a Printer Style:

1. **Choose File⇨Print (Ctrl+P).**

   The Print Document dialog box appears.

2. **Make any adjustments or changes to the dialog box, and to the boxes that appear by clicking the Paper, Options, Color, and Features buttons.**

3. **Press the Ctrl key.**

   The Print button in the Print Document dialog box changes to the word Styles (**Figure 16**).

4. **Click the Styles button.**

   Be sure to keep the Ctrl key pressed while you click. The Rename Printer Style dialog box appears (**Figure 17**).

5. **Name your Printer Style and click the OK button.**

   Your new Printer Style, which contains all the information in the Print Document dialog boxes when you saved it, can be chosen from the Printer Styles submenu in the File menu (**Figure 18**).

Creating Printer Styles

To enlarge your printout:

1. **Choose File⇨Print (Ctrl+P).**
   The Print Document dialog box appears (**Figure 19**).

2. **Click the Paper button.**
   The Print Paper dialog box appears (**Figure 20**).

3. **In the Scale box, enter a percentage greater than 100%.**
   I entered 150% in this example. The blue lines in the diagram (hard, if not impossible, to see here), show where the real edges of the page are (this can be important, in case the edges of the page extend beyond the edges of the paper you're printing to).

To reduce your printout:

1. **Choose File⇨Print (Ctrl+P).**
   The Print Document dialog box appears.

2. **Click the Paper button.**
   The Print Paper dialog box appears.

3. **In the Scale box, enter a percentage less than 100%.**
   I entered 50% in this example. The blue lines in the diagram show where the real edges of the page are. In this case (**Figure 21**), the edges are inset from the edges of the paper by a few inches.

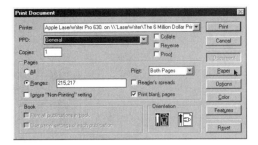

Figure 19. Click the Paper button in the Print Document dialog box.

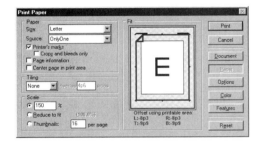

Figure 20. When you enter a Scale value greater than 100%, the edges of the document (represented here by dark lines) can go beyond the edge of the paper you're printing to.

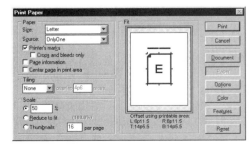

Figure 21. The page has been set to print at 50% of its actual size.

Enlarging and Reducing Printouts

Trapping

When you've created a document that uses multiple colors, especially spot colors, you always run the risk of gaps appearing between where those colors are supposed to butt up against each other. This isn't a limitation of PageMaker (objects are positioned *exactly* within PageMaker and when printed), but is instead due to the variation which occurs on almost all commercial printing presses. A slight fraction of an inch slip of alignment of a plate on a printing press, and disaster can strike.

There are all sorts of ways to "cheat" and to trap from your end, whether you're in PageMaker or Illustrator. But your best bet is to talk to your commercial printer before you do anything. This will allow you to find out what kind of trapping (if any) you should do to your document. Many commercial printers will take your electronic files, and output them themselves or get a service bureau to do that for them. If this is the case, they can make the adjustments for you.

I've found that most commercial printers would rather make the changes themselves, than to have an inexperienced person attempt them. If the trapping is off, it could waste quite a bit of film and press time, resulting in higher costs for your printer (and you, eventually).

Trapping and Joe Desktop Publisher

To trap in PageMaker:

1. **Choose File ⇨ Preferences ⇨ Trapping (Figure 22).**

   The Trapping Preferences dialog box appears, with all sorts of confusing information in it (**Figure 23**).

2. **Talk to your commercial printer about what values, if any, to change in the Trapping Preferences dialog box.**

   This can't be emphasized enough. Each printer has different presses with different needs, so don't take what one printer says and use it for a job that's going to be printed by his cross-town rival.

3. **Enter the values and make the changes in the Trapping Preferences dialog box that were recommended by your printer.**

   Trapping is too important to be creative, so use exactly the values you were given.

4. **Click the OK button and save the document.**

   Those trapping preferences are saved with your document.

   Now when the document is printed with separations, the trapping values you've entered will be in effect.

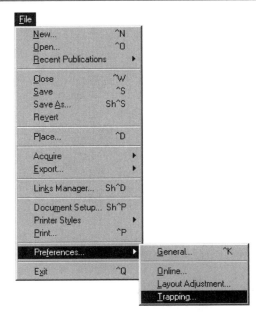

Figure 22. Choose Trapping from the Preferences submenu in the File menu.

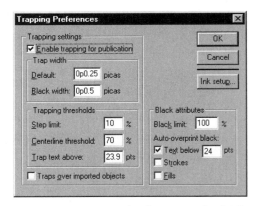

Figure 23. Be afraid. Be very afraid. The Trapping Preferences dialog box.

PART VI

APPENDIXES

The terms on these pages are those you'll run into while using PageMaker and related desktop publishing and graphics software.

Actual Size: The onscreen size of your document which most closely resembles the size of actual output.

Adobe Illustrator: The leading graphics drawing package from Adobe Systems. It shares a similar interface to PageMaker.

Adobe Photoshop: The industry standard pixel-based image manipulation software.

Adobe Type Manager: Software that makes text look good at almost any point size. ATM 4.0 includes anti-aliasing capabilities.

Alignment: How text is positioned horizontally. For example, flush left means that all text is aligned along the left edge of the text block.

All Caps: A character-based style that changes all lowercase letters to uppercase (capital) letters.

Ascender: The section of a lowercase character that extends upward above the X-height of the character.

Baseline: The bottom of a lowercase character, such as all the letters in this definition.

Bleed: Artwork or text that extends off the edge of a printed page.

Body Copy: Text that appears throughout a publication. Usually a style that other styles are based upon.

Bold: A character attribute that makes characters appear thicker and heavier.

Bounding Box: A box that defines the rectangular area of any object. You can view the bounding box of any object by grouping it.

Checkbox: The square to the left of certain commands in dialog boxes. If active, the box contains an X.

Clipboard: The place that stores objects and text that are copied or cut.

CMYK: Cyan, Magenta, Yellow and Black. Commonly referred to as process colors.

Color Separations: The individual sheets that are printed for each color in a document.

Columns: Vertical boxes that contain text on a single page.

Constrain: To confine the movement of an object to 45° angles, or to confine the sizing to exact proportions.

Control Palette: The palette along the bottom (usually) of the screen, where text and objects can be quickly modified.

Copy: To select an object and place a duplicate of it on the clipboard, so it can be pasted later.

Crop: To remove a portion of the image by dragging the cropping tool on one of the image's sizing handles.

Descender: The portion of a character that extends below the baseline.

Desktop Publishing: The use of a personal computer to create text, graphics, and layout. PageMaker pioneered the field in the 1980s.

Dialog Box: A box that appears in PageMaker requiring you to enter information or confirm an activity.

DPI: Dots Per Inch. The resolution of an output device. Most laser printers are 300 or 600 dpi.

Ellipse: An oval created with PageMaker's Ellipse tool.

EPS: Encapsulated PostScript. A self-contained graphic file optimized for PostScript printing.

Fill: The inside of one of PageMaker's drawing objects.

Folio: Headers or footers at the top and bottom, respectively, of each page in a document. Commonly placed on master pages.

Font: A set of characters with a similar appearance, designed to be used together.

Grayscale: An image with no color, but 256 levels of gray.

Greeked Text: Text that appears as gray bars in PageMaker due to its small size.

Group: Several objects that are linked together so that when one is selected, the others are selected as well.

Gutter: The space between columns.

Hinting: Intelligent font attributes that cause them to display better at small sizes and low resolutions.

Horizontal Scale: The width of a character; the default is 100%.

HyperLinks: See Links, (2).

Hyphenation: How words are split at the ends of lines.

Indent: The distance from the left or right edges of a text block to the text.

Italic: A curved, slanted style of a font.

Justified: Text that is aligned to both the left and right edges of a text block.

Kern: To remove or add space between two characters.

Landscape: A document whose width is greater than its height.

Layers: Portions of a document that can be hidden or locked independently of the rest of the document.

Leading: The amount of space between baselines.

Line Break: The end of a line of text, created either automatically by text wrapping or manually by inserting a special character.

Links: (1) The location of placed objects in a PageMaker file. (2) Hot spots in a PageMaker document that allow you to quickly go somewhere else (referred to in PageMaker as HyperLinks).

Margin: The distance from the edge of the page to the area where text and graphics are.

Marquee: A dotted line that appears when you drag with the Pointer tool.

Menu Bar: The list of commands along the top of the PageMaker screen.

Object: Any text block, PageMaker graphical element, or placed image.

Origin Point: The static corner or side of any object that doesn't move when transformed.

Palette: A movable, floating window that contains oft-used commands.

Pasteboard: The area in a document outside the page boundaries.

PICT: A common screen graphics format, useful for documents that won't be printed.

Place: The process of importing an image into PageMaker.

PostScript: A page description language developed by Adobe which is present in most laser printers.

Printer's Marks: Crop marks, registration marks, color bars, and other text and symbols used by printers to control how a document appears on a printing press.

Process Color: See CMYK.

Resolution: The number of dots that exists in one horizontal inch of an output or viewing device. See DPI.

Reverse: A character attribute that changes black text to white.

RGB: Red, Green, and Blue. The colors that make up graphics that should be used for onscreen purposes.

Rotate: To spin an object around a certain point by a certain angle.

Rulers: Onscreen measurement devices that appear along the top and left of the document window.

Select: To click on an item so that it can be modified in some way.

Separations: Individual printed sheets for each color in a document.

Spot Color: A color that will be printed with a special colored ink on a separate plate from PageMaker.

Stroke: The border of an object in PageMaker.

TIFF: Tagged Image File Format. A common format for pixel-based placed images.

Tint: A percentage of a color.

Toolbox: The floating palette that contains all of PageMaker's tools.

Tracking: The process of adding or removing space between characters.

Trapping: The process of ensuring that no white gaps will exist between abutting colors when a document is printed.

White Space: Empty space in a document.

WYSIWYG: A tacky phrase used in the 1980s to describe PageMaker's onscreen display: What You See Is What You Get.

Zoom: To magnify a certain portion of a document onscreen.

What's New in PageMaker 6.5

PageMaker has gone through all sorts of changes since it was first introduced more than ten years ago from a little startup company called Aldus.

PageMaker has been the standard page layout software program for Windows ever since it overtook Ventura Publisher almost eight years ago. The last two releases of PageMaker have drastically upped the features of the software, as these releases are becoming more and more like other successful Adobe products. The changes from version 6.0 to 6.5 may seem cosmetic, but a lot of hidden functionality was stashed into this release, especially extended Web and PDF support.

What's New in PageMaker 6.5

Web-ready features

HTML Export plug-in: Exporting to HTML preserves most of the PageMaker layout and hyperlinks.

Hyperlinks: Links to locations within and outside the PageMaker document are supported, via the new Hyperlinks palette (**Figure 1**).

Automatic Image Conversion: Exported images are automatically converted to JPEG or GIF format.

Advanced PDF Support: PageMaker allows embedded links for PDF documents.

Figure 1. The Hyperlinks palette.

Layout features

Layers: The new Layers palette (**Figure 2**) allows you to organize your artwork better than ever before.

Frames: Text can now be placed in semi-static frames instead of just windowshade text blocks.

Multiple Master Pages: Using the new Master Pages palette (**Figure 3**), you can define as many Master pages as you need in a single document.

Freeform Polygon tool: The new polygon tool allows you to draw irregular shapes.

Automatic Layout Adjustment: Change layouts when you change page size automatically.

Photoshop Filter support: Apply Photoshop filters to placed pixel-based images.

Illustrator Native file support: Import Illustrator files in native format.

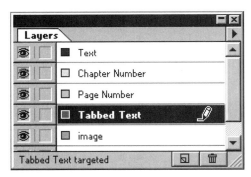

Figure 2. The Layers palette.

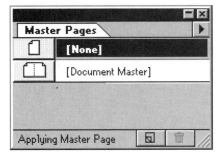

Figure 3. The Master Pages palette.

PageTools is such an important part of my PageMaker usage that I feel PageMaker is incomplete without it. From PageBars, which provide one-click access to every menu item within PageMaker, to PageMarks, which automatically draws crop marks around any selected object, PageTools has something for everyone. In my case, it has a lot of somethings.

Extensis is pretty good about trying before buying as well; they offer a 30-day free trial during which time every PageTools component is fully functional. If you decide you like it, send in your money, and the software works from that point on. You can even download the software from their web site at www.extensis.com.

Introduction to Extensis PageTools 2.0

The PageTools button bars

When you first install PageTools, you'll notice a button bar (called a PageBar) along the top of your screen, under the menu bar. You'll also notice a floating palette with buttons on it.

The bar along the top of the screen is the standard bar (**Figure 1**), which contains buttons for such common activities as creating a new document, saving, spell checking, grouping and ungrouping, and others.

The floating toolbar (**Figure 2**), called PageTools, contains buttons for each of the PageTools components.

You can also access the PageTools components by choosing Utilities ➪ Plug-Ins ➪PageWhatever, but this is much more difficult than clicking on a button.

Figure 1. The standard toolbar that appears when you launch PageMaker with PageTools for the first time.

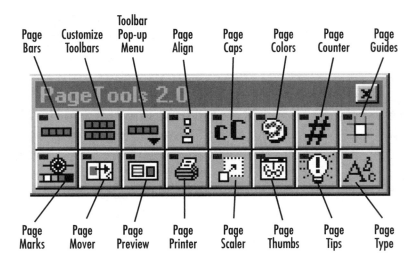

Figure 2. The PageTools button bar.

Figure 3. Click on the Customize Toolbars button in the PageTools button bar.

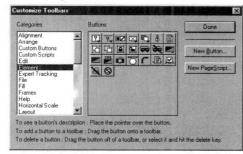

Figure 4. The Customize Toolbars dialog box, showing the Element category buttons.

Figure 5. Drag a button outside the dialog box and you've created a button bar.

Figure 6. A toolbar full of buttons I created in just a few minutes.

You can quickly create a customized button bar full of buttons that correspond to functions you frequently use.

To create a custom toolbar:

1. **Click the Customize Toolbars button on the PageTools bar (Figure 3).**

   The Customize Toolbars dialog box appears (**Figure 4**).

2. **Select a category from which you'd like to create a button.**

   I've selected the Element category for this example.

3. **Drag a button out of the dialog box onto your document.**

   It will become a tiny little floating palette with one button on it (**Figure 5**).

4. **Repeat Steps 2 and 3, dragging the additional buttons on top of the existing palette, until you have a button bar full of buttons you want to use.**

   Figure 6 shows a button bar I created in just a few minutes.

TIPS AND TRICKS

You can adjust buttons within button bars by Ctrl+dragging them down or to the right. This allows you to change their location, as well as to insert space between any two buttons.

Creating Your Own Button Bar

PageCaps

PageCaps provides a powerful way to quickly change the case of selected letters. The Title caps function is extremely powerful, as it has a built-in dictionary for words that are capitalized in special ways (like "McDonald's" or "PageMaker").

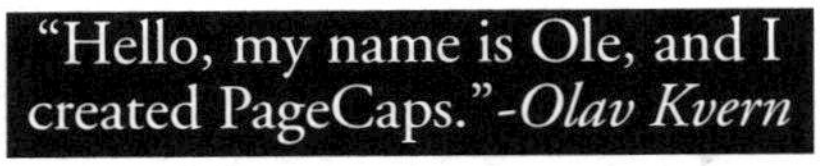

To use PageCaps:

1. Select the letters whose case you would like to change (**Figure** 7).

2. Click the PageCaps button on the PageTools button bar (**Figure** 8).

   The PageCaps dialog box appears (**Figure** 9).

3. Choose the type of capitalization you would like to use (see chart below) and click the Apply button.

   The text you selected will be adjusted to reflect the case change you specified (**Figure** 10).

4. Click the Done button to exit the dialog box.

PageCaps options

You can choose from the following options which look like these sentences:

this is lowercase via pagecaps.

THIS IS UPPERCASE VIA PAGECAPS.

This is sentence caps via pagecaps.

This Is Title Caps Via Pagecaps.

This iS raNdOMcAPs VIa PagECaps.

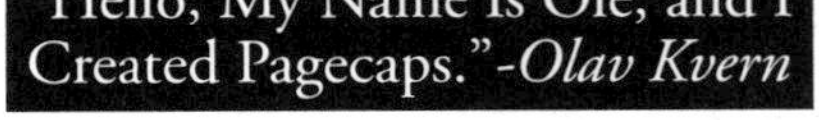

Figure 7. Select the characters which you would like to change. I selected this entire sentence.

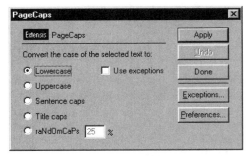

Figure 8. Click the PageCaps button on the PageTools button bar.

Figure 9. The PageCaps dialog box.

"Hello, My Name Is Ole, and I Created Pagecaps."-*Olav Kvern*

Figure 10. The text from Figure 7 after applying Title caps to it, using the built in exceptions. You could add an exception that makes Pagecaps appear as PageCaps automatically.

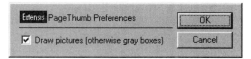

Figure 11. Click the PageThumb button on the PageTools button bar.

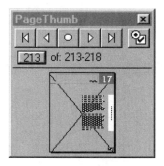

Figure 12. The PageThumb palette showing the first page of a chapter.

Figure 13. PageThumb Preferences.

PageThumb

PageThumb is a handy little palette that you can use to navigate around PageMaker documents. It's resizable and fairly quick, making going to a certain page a simple process of clicking on the page.

To use PageThumb:

1. **Click the PageThumb button on the PageTools button bar (Figure 11).**

   The PageThumb palette appears (**Figure 12**).

2. **Click on the page you wish to go to.**

   PageMaker zips to that page.

PageThumb options

By clicking on the little preferences button in the upper right of the PageThumbs palette, you can turn on and off a few different options (**Figure 13**).

Draw thumbnails faster greeks text with gray bars.

Draw high resolution text is what's shown in **Figure 12**.

Draw pictures creates miniature versions of the images on each page.

I usually work with Draw thumbnails faster checked and Draw pictures off. This gives me almost no slowdown whatsoever.

Navigating with PageThumb

PageAlign

PageAlign is a component that's been part of PageTools since before PageMaker had an Align function. For the most part, the align and distribution functions in PageAlign match exactly what you can do with PageMaker's Element⇨Align function. But what PageTools has that PageMaker doesn't is button bars. Using the built-in PageAlign toolbar can save you loads of time, especially if you're like me and you only use one or two of the alignment functions. I used the vertical distribute option for images and captions (after I grouped them) for each page of this book.

To use the PageAlign button bar:

1. **Click the PageBars button on the PageTools palette (Figure 14).**

   The PageBars window appears (**Figure 15**).

2. **Click to the left of the PageAlign toolbar.**

   The PageAlign toolbar will appear in the PageMaker window (**Figure 16**).

3. **Click the Done button.**

   You can now use the PageAlign features simply by clicking on the appropriate buttons.

Figure 14. *Click the PageBars button on the PageTools palette.*

Figure 15. *Click to the left of the PageAlign entry in the PageBars dialog box.*

Figure 16. *The PageAlign toolbar, ready to use.*

Figure 17. Click the PageType button in the PageTools palette.

Figure 18. The PageType palette.

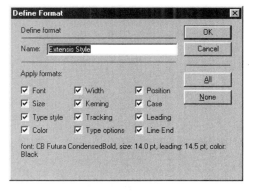

Figure 19. The Define Format dialog box.

Figure 20. The new format will be added to the list of formats in the PageType palette.

PageType

PageType styles text in all sorts of ways with just a click, without affecting an entire paragraph. PageMaker's built-in styles are wonderful, but they affect an entire paragraph at a time. If you need to change one or two words in a paragraph to a different font, and maybe add some basic character attribute styling such as baseline shift, horizontal scale, and underline, you would have to select the words you want to change and apply each of these attributes individually in PageMaker.

PageType takes this ugly drudgery away by allowing you to change multiple attributes with a single keystroke.

To create a PageType format:

1. **Click the PageType button on the PageTools palette (Figure 17).**
   The PageType palette appears (**Figure 18**).

2. **Select the formatted text from which you wish to create the format.**

3. **Click the + button.**
   The Define Format dialog box appears (**Figure 19**).

4. **Enter the name of the format.**

5. **Choose which attributes to include with the format and click the OK button.**
   A new format will be added to the list in the PageType palette (**Figure 20**).

Using PageType

273

D

Index P

Index T-U